Riding into Glory

An Introduction to the Battle of the Little Bighorn

By Bob Snelson

Snelsonbooks.com

Cover art "Yellow Nose" courtesy of Ralph Allen Heinz

Cover design by Michael Schnobrich

ISBN 0-9723935-4-4

Copyright 2004 by Robert R. Snelson

All rights reserved. No part of this publication may be reproduced, stored in a retrieval system, or transmitted, in any form, or by any means, electronic, mechanical, photocopying, recording, or otherwise, without the prior consent of the publisher. Printed in the United States of America.

Acknowledgments

I would like to thank Joan Croy from Little Big Horn Associates for first suggesting this book, getting permission for the use of the cover art, providing me with a key photograph and her friendship. Many thanks to Ralph Allen Heinz for allowing me to use his painting "Yellow Nose" for the cover. Danielle Chiroux for talking me into taking on the project, editing the manuscript, her tremendous love and support that I dearly needed. Mike Schnobrich for once again taking care of my graphics and book cover. I would also like to thank James J. Dulemba of Old West Historic Images for providing many of the photographs. I would like to thank the staff of the Little Bighorn Battlefield National Monument for the use of many of the photographs and their efforts to preserve the battlefield. Special thanks go to Dr. Jeffrey Broome for his friendship, suggestions and support for this book.

Table of Contents

Preface	2
I. Basics of the Indian Wars	4
II. The Crow's Nest	23
III. The Valley Fight	37
IV. Custer Moves North	56
V. Benteen and the Pack Train	63
VI. Medicine Tail Coulee	75
VII. The Keogh Fight	83
VIII. The Last Stand	99
IX. Weir Point	114
X. The Hilltop Fight	126
XI. Day Two	133
XII. Aftermath	146
Glossary	161
Index	167

Preface

Many books have been written about the Battle of the Little Bighorn. However, few have been written for the purpose of introducing younger readers to the subject. Unless we take the time to teach future generations about our history, it will quickly be forgotten. We owe our ancestors a debt of gratitude that can only be repaid by remembering them and the hardships they endured in order to make this country what it is today. In doing so, younger generations will learn to respect those ancestors as well.

We should not attempt to judge others by their race, color or religion. Each has its guilty and innocent, good and evil. This book was not written for the purpose of apologizing for the wrongs committed by either of the civilizations represented in this book, white or red. Life on the nineteenth century American frontier was perilous and it required tough people to survive. A simple moment of carelessness often resulted in death. To sit in our safe living rooms and attempt to judge how people behaved on the dangerous frontier more than a century ago would be foolish.

We should understand that it sometimes required a great deal of work and luck for our ancestors to survive each day on the frontier. Food had to be grown or hunted because stores were virtually nonexistent. There was no one to stand guard while the farmers plowed their fields or when the cowboy tended to his herd of cattle.

The officers of the frontier Army found that as a rule the Indians they fought seldom changed their tactics in battle. In chapter one, we will discuss those tactics and their importance in determining the course and outcome of the battle. As we shall learn, there are also exceptions to just about every rule as the Army found out during the summer of 1876.

As I relate the story of the battle you should keep in mind that there are still many mysteries surrounding this battle. For instance, we can only guess as to what happened on some areas of the battlefield. We can't even be sure how many Indian warriors took part in the battle. The bones of some of the soldiers have never been discovered and many that were found were never positively identified. Maybe some of these mysteries will be solved by someone who is reading about this battle for the first time.

I. Basics of the Indian Wars

Before getting into the battle itself, we must first be able to grasp some basic realities of the Indian wars. Most, if not all of these realities were known to Brevet Major General George Armstrong Custer, the field commander of the Seventh Cavalry. In ten years on the western plains, he experienced most of these realities first-hand. While he only fought in two small battles with the Sioux and Cheyenne he spent a great deal of time chasing them. The decisions he made en route to the Little Bighorn River and during the battle itself were based on this knowledge and experience.

Nineteenth century warfare was much different than what we see today. Communications between army detachments were accomplished through trumpets or by courier, neither of which were reliable for passing detailed instructions in a timely manner. Maps of the frontier regions were inaccurate and incomplete, giving little or no terrain details. Transportation consisted of horses, mules and wagons. A cavalryman could only travel as far and as fast as his horse could carry him.

After the American Civil War, the Army suffered a reduction in force typical after most large scale military conflicts. The cost of maintaining a large standing army after an expensive war was too steep for the government to maintain. Most of the Army's officers and enlisted men were discharged from further service. During the Civil War the American Union Army numbered in the hundreds of thousands. Only about twenty-five thousand men remained in the Army after the war. The relatively few regiments that remained in existence were spread out across the United States; insufficient in number for patrolling the lonely outposts of the American West.

Many officers on the frontier had commanded brigades or regiments during the Civil War. They had been awarded brevet or honorary ranks in order for them to command such large numbers of men. After the war they found themselves commanding a company of men instead of the much larger units they led during the war. Consequently, their ranks were also reduced to reflect the reduced size of their new commands.

For instance, General Custer had attained the brevet rank of Major General during the Civil War. His command of a cavalry division merited him such a rank. However, most of the regiments under his command were volunteer state militias that were disbanded at the conclusion of the war. After the war there was no longer a need for that division of cavalry or the man to command it. Following a reorganization of the Army, Custer was assigned the regular Army rank of Lieutenant Colonel. He held this rank until his death at the Little Bighorn River in 1876. Due to his brevet rank, Custer was often referred to as General Custer. To avoid confusion we shall do so as well.

Men returning from the war, from both the North and South, found that they had outgrown their former ways of life or had nothing to return home to. The American Civil War and the westward expansion would also prove to change the lives of the American Indians. Many settlers began to move west in search of new opportunities for themselves and their families. This, in turn, angered the plains' tribes whose lands were being crossed and/or settled upon by the migrating American and European immigrants.

The problem between the white settlers and the Indians lay in two societies with opposite viewpoints on just about everything. The two cultures could not continue to coexist without continuous trouble because both parties had things that the other wanted. The settlers wanted land and the Indians wanted guns and other goods that they could not produce themselves. Neither side respected the property ownership of the other so they had a tendency to steal and murder to get what they wanted.

Peace treaties were usually doomed from the start and failed to stop the fighting for very long. Peace commissions were assigned to negotiate treaties with the Indian tribes. However, no treaties were valid until approved by Congress, which rarely did so without first making at least some changes. It is doubtful that the tribal leaders would have been informed of the unofficial status of their copy of any treaty, not that they could have read it anyway. They might not even be informed of the changes made by Congress until they had violated the new terms of the ratified treaty. It is no wonder they considered the peace commissioners to be liars.

Similarly, the young warriors of the tribes often disagreed with their leaders who wished to sign the treaties. Indian tribes were male dominated societies where the young men were expected to become warriors. A warrior generally ranged in age from about 15 to 38 years of age. The usual way for young warriors to gain prestige was to fight with and steal from the white settlers or other tribes.

A young man could not become a respected warrior if the tribe had no enemies to fight or to steal horses from. It was not unusual for young warriors to slip away from their camps to go on raids because the old chiefs had no power to stop them. In retaliation for the raids the government would usually punish the whole tribe by refusing to issue the goods (food, guns, ammunition and blankets) that were promised in the treaties.

When white hunters began slaughtering the buffalo for their hides, they were often hunting on land set aside for the Indians by treaty. This eventually resulted in starvation for the Plains Indians since the buffalo was their primary source of food. The United States government generally ignored the treaty violations by the white buffalo hunters because it would eventually make the Indian tribes dependent on the government when their source of food ran out. The government could then force the Indians to live on the reservations created for them. Treaties were thus violated by both the whites and the Indians making warfare between the two cultures inevitable.

The frontier Army was too ill equipped and few in number to protect settlers or stop treaty violators of either race. Until 1876, the Seventh Cavalry was never united as a regiment sized force. This was typical of all the regiments in the Army. For the frontier Army, everything was in short supply except harsh conditions, poor food and boredom, relieved only by the occasional horrifying prospect of being mutilated by hostile warriors. Promotions were scarce and required the death or retirement of superiors. The scarcity of promotions and the reduction from their temporary ranks often led to disloyalty and jealousy amongst the officers. An Army requires discipline and cooperation in order to be successful.

Post Civil War soldiers received little real training and were treated poorly by many of their officers. Their diets generally consisted of a small ration of salted pork and hard tack (a large thick cracker). The enlisted men were often poor immigrants who spoke little, if any English. Most came from Ireland, Germany and Italy.

The first problem associated with warfare against the Plains Indians was in finding them and forcing them to stay and fight. The advantage of speed and mobility rested entirely with the Indians. George Bent, the son of fur trader William Bent and the Cheyenne named Owl Woman, said it best, "The troops could reach the Indians only when it suited the latter to risk an engagement, and this happened but seldom."[1] There were some exceptions to this rule, but they took a mixture of skill and luck to achieve.

The Plains Indians were nomads that traveled light, carrying little that was not essential. They hunted and gathered their food as they found it, trusting in nature to provide for their needs. The buffalo was their version of a Super Wal-Mart, providing virtually everything they required including food, clothing, shelter, cooking utensils, religious items and fuel for fires.

The Army required slow moving wagons and mules to carry their supplies to the battlefield, which was typically the Indians' own backyard. They had to carry their food with them as they had little opportunity to hunt while they searched for hostile Indians. They also carried grain to supplement the diets of the large Army horses. The ideal amount of forage (food) for cavalry mounts in garrison was fourteen pounds of hay and twelve pounds of grain per day.² It was impossible for the Army to supply their cavalry with anything close to the ideal amount of forage for their horses during a campaign. Consequently, the cavalry horses would grow weaker by the day as they chased the elusive warriors.

By contrast, the smaller Indian ponies thrived on the spring and summer grasses of the plains. They were not required to carry heavy loads like their Army counterparts, and the Indians generally owned more than one pony, putting less strain on each animal. It should now be easier to understand why the Army had so much trouble catching up to the Indians.

The weakest time of year for the Indian tribes was the winter months when the grass was poor and would barely sustain the pony herds. This made the villages less mobile and easier to surprise as the Indians spent more hours of each day in their lodges. The tribes were less wary during these months of bitterly cold weather. They did not expect the soldiers to be searching for them during days of below zero temperatures and blizzards.

The enlistments of scouts such as Mitch Boyer (also spelled Bouyer), Frank Grouard, Baptiste "Big Bat" Pourier and William F. Cody were instrumental in improving the Army's ability to find the elusive villages. These noted frontier scouts often learned from the friendly Indian tribes they often lived with. Their knowledge of the frontier geography gave them the ability to locate the favorite camping locations of the hostile tribes.

When the soldiers were able to locate a hostile village, the warriors would stand and fight the soldiers while their non-combatants (women, children, and elderly) fled with whatever they could carry. When the non-combatants were safely out of harm's way the warriors would retreat in several directions, leaving too many trails for the soldiers to follow.

The Indian warriors fought as individuals and were not required to follow orders from their chiefs during a battle. "If some aggressive war was contemplated, these chiefs agreed upon the plans. But when any battle actually began it was a case of every man for himself."[3] A warrior typically followed other, more respected warriors into battle but could pick and choose where he would make his own fight. Sometimes this was effective, but most often, it would lead to a total lack of cooperation necessary to win a pitched battle.[4]

The war leaders were responsible to the village for making sure that the warriors did not throw their lives away recklessly. If too many warriors were killed, the leader would be held accountable by the village.[5] The Army could replace its combat losses with new recruits while it would take a generation to replace a warrior. With that knowledge, it is easy to understand why the Indians were not keen on fighting prolonged battles with their enemies.

The Indians' reluctance to fight conventional battles against the better armed soldiers was often mistaken for cowardice. However, when their families or village were threatened most warriors would fight to the death rather than surrender or retreat. They also fought more tenaciously when victory seemed assured.[6] When an enemy turned their backs to run away they were easier to kill. A favorite tactic of most tribes was the ambush. While many whites believed that Indians were ignorant savages, they often proved to be quite ingenious in planning ambushes and avoiding the Army.

Neither the average soldier nor the average warrior was an accomplished marksman. The Army did not provide enough ammunition for training purposes. Commanders were forced to horde their limited supply of ammunition for combat purposes only.[7] The warriors did not have a steady supply of rifles or ammunition. They had to take them from those they killed, buy them at extremely high prices from corrupt traders or bargain for them as part of treaty agreements. Consequently, battles between soldiers and warriors might consist of thousands of bullets being fired with only a dozen or so casualties on each side.

During the Battle of the Little Bighorn, the officers and men of the Seventh Cavalry carried the Springfield Carbine, Model 1873 and the Colt Single Action Army Revolver, Model 1873. The Springfield weighed about seven pounds and measured forty-one inches in length. An experienced trooper could fire it twelve to fifteen times per minute (rate of fire). Its most accurate firing distance (effective range) was less than three hundred yards but an experienced marksman could hit a target with some consistency at up to six hundred yards. While it lacked the rate of fire of the seventeen-shot Henry and Winchester lever action rifles, it had superior range. The lever action rifles lost a great deal of their accuracy past one hundred yards.[8]

Soldiers were allowed to carry other weapons if they wanted to at their own expense, but few opted to do so. Soldiers received little money for their military service and could rarely afford more expensive guns. General Custer carried a Remington .50 caliber rolling block sporting rifle with octagonal barrel and two Webley British Bulldog double-action revolvers. Captain Thomas French, the commander of Company M, carried a .50 caliber Springfield rifle, known as a Long Tom. First Sergeant John Ryan of M Company carried a .45 caliber Sharps telescopic rifle that had been specially made for him.[9]

The Indians carried a variety of different weapons including Sharps, Henrys, Winchesters, Remingtons, Ballards, Maynards, Spencers, Enfields, Colts and Springfields.[10] Some carried rifles while others had only pistols. Many had no firearms and used the bow and arrow. War clubs, tomahawks and lances were also used. As soldiers were killed during the battle, the warriors were able to increase their number of weapons and acquire a good supply of ammunition.

The warriors' use of cover (protection from bullets) and concealment (hiding) in battle was a significant factor in their low casualty rates. Their practice of recovering the bodies of their dead made an accurate estimate of warrior casualties impossible. Therefore, the Army would grossly exaggerate the number of casualties they had inflicted on the warriors.

The Indians generally wouldn't risk a long fight if the spoils of victory would not be worth the possible loss of warriors. The American Indian did not believe in the "attack at all costs" style of warfare as some modern armies do. They could not afford the loss of warriors that they might incur if they attempted to kill all of their enemies.

Now you should understand Indian warfare as General Custer had experienced it. He, like most other officers, found it almost impossible to get the Indians to stand and fight against anything close to a regiment sized unit. For that reason, Custer probably had little respect for the Indians as a military force, although he respected their skills as individual fighters, hunters and trackers.

Before we get into the narrative of the battle, we should keep in mind that the actual military goal of the

1876 campaign was to force all of the Sioux and Cheyenne Indians onto the reservations once and for all. The soldiers were not expected to kill them all. They were only expected to kill any Indians that refused to go to the reservation. The Sioux Nation consisted of the following sub-tribes; Blackfoot, Brule, Hunkpapa, Minniconjou, Oglala, Sans Arc, Santee and Two Kettle. The Sioux were allied with the Arapaho, Northern Cheyenne and Southern Cheyenne tribes.

As the battle unfolds in the following chapters, you should be able to grasp why some of the seemingly stranger decisions were made. I have broken down the chapters to cover essential elements of the battle or to describe the activities of the detachments of the Seventh Cavalry. Keep in mind that the actions of the various detachments of the Seventh Cavalry often occurred simultaneously even though they are described in separate chapters. Chapters 6 through 8 concern the five companies with General Custer. Since there were no Army survivors from this segment of the battle, we can only speculate on their actions based on our interpretations of Indian accounts and archeological studies. These chapters are the author's interpretation of those events.

[1] George E. Hyde, Life of George Bent, pp. 295

[2] Daniel O. Magnussen, Peter Thompson's Narrative of the Little Bighorn Campaign, 1876, pp. 76

[3] Thomas B. Marquis, Wooden Leg, A Warrior Who Fought Custer, pp. 119

[4] Hyde, pp. 170-171, 294

[5] Marquis, Keep the Last Bullet For Yourself, pp. 68

[6] Don Rickey, Jr., Forty Miles A Day On Beans and Hay, pp 283

[7] Ibid, pp 86, 99-101

[8] Terry Schulman, Guns of the Little Bighorn, Wild West magazine, June 1998

[9] Ibid

[10] Ibid

The Black Hills Expedition of 1874. This is a perfect example of how difficult it was for the army to travel with its supplies. Picture courtesy of the National Archives.

The Super Wal-Mart of the American Plains Indian tribes. Buffalo provided for almost all of their needs. Courtesy Denver Public Library.

Brevet Major General George Armstrong Custer. Commanded the 7th Cavalry at the Little Bighorn. Often accused of being a reckless glory hunter, his courage was unquestioned and his tactical abilities underrated. Courtesy of LBHBNM.

Sitting Bull famed Hunkpapa Sioux civic leader. He was more valuable to his people when providing advice and inspiration rather than as a fighter. Courtesy of James Dulemba.

Settlers like these moved across or settled upon lands hunted by the Plains Indian tribes causing friction between the two civilizations. These settlers often became the targets of raiding parties who wanted guns, ammunition, sugar, coffee and other goods that were desired by the tribes. Courtesy of the Denver Public Library.

II. The Crow's Nest

At dawn on the 25th of June, 1876, Lieutenant Charles Varnum, Chief of Scouts for General George A. Custer, was awakened from a short nap by one of the Crow Indian scouts under his command. Lieutenant Varnum and his Indian scouts were searching for a large, hostile Sioux village. Any Sioux found away from their assigned reservation were considered to be hostile.

He was directed to look toward the Little Bighorn River, approximately fifteen miles to the west. The scouts informed him of the massive pony herds and the smoke from the cook fires which indicated a large village. The village itself was hidden from view due to some large bluffs that lay between Lieutenant Varnum and the village.

Lieutenant Varnum could see nothing of the pony herds or the village with his tired, untrained eyes. He was told to look for "worms moving" but still could see nothing from his position at the Crow's Nest. This was an Indian lookout position on high ground that afforded a view into the Little Bighorn Valley. He wrote a message to General Custer informing him of what the scouts had observed. The message was entrusted to two Arikara Indian scouts, Red Star and Bull. They were to deliver it to Custer who was with the rest of his regiment.[1]

The two scouts had no trouble locating General Custer's camp because he had allowed the men to build cooking fires to boil coffee. Lieutenant Varnum and the other scouts also observed the smoke. A small group of mounted Sioux warriors were soon seen in the near distance. It quickly became apparent that these warriors were heading in the direction of Custer's camp which they could not miss and would undoubtedly, report to the hostile village. An attempt was made to intercept and kill these warriors but was aborted when the warriors altered their course slightly.[2]

While awaiting word from Lieutenant Varnum, General Custer was in camp discussing the upcoming battle with his trusted scout Bloody Knife who was half Sioux and half Arikara. Many of the other Arikara scouts were present as well. Bloody Knife informed General Custer that they would find enough Sioux to keep them fighting for two or three days. Custer reportedly smiled and said, "I guess we'll get through them in one day." What Bloody

Knife may have realized, that the General didn't, was that the multiple trails intersecting the large one they had been following were converging trails, not diverging trails. In simple terms, more Indians were joining the already large village, not leaving it, as Custer may have believed.[3]

After receiving Lieutenant Varnum's message, General Custer mounted a horse and went to the Crow's Nest to see for himself. He was joined by an orderly trumpeter, Arikara interpreter Fred Gerard, Bloody Knife, and the Arikara scouts Red Star, Bob-Tailed Bull and Little Brave.[4] The rest of the regiment followed shortly after, minus Sergeant William Curtiss and two privates from Company F. These three soldiers traveled back the way they had come during the previous night's march to retrieve some clothing and a large crate of hard tack that had fallen from one of the pack mules. The soldiers found the missing items with a few hostile warriors who were busy checking the contents of the box.[5]

The two groups began shooting at each other and soon retreated without casualties. The soldiers never recovered the clothing or food. The sergeant reported the contact to Captain George Yates, commander of Company F, at the column's next halt which was one mile to the west of the Crow's Nest. What nobody present knew until much later was that these Indians were from Little Wolf's small Cheyenne village of seven lodges. They had been traveling behind the column for the past day attempting to join the large village that the soldiers were searching for.[6]

At the Crow's Nest, Custer was unable to see any signs of the village. According to Lieutenant Varnum, General Custer and the noted frontier scout, Mitch Boyer, had a small disagreement regarding the location and size of the village. Custer had expressed some doubt as to whether there was really a Sioux village in the Little Bighorn Valley.[7] The scouts and General Custer returned to the column of soldiers which were now ahead of them. Custer was informed of Sergeant Curtiss' brief skirmish and of the warriors watching the troops from the surrounding ridges. The time was about 10:30 a.m.

General Custer's plan to attack on the morning of the 26th was now in a shambles since the Sioux and Cheyenne had become aware of the closeness of the soldiers. He convened a hasty officer's call and informed them of his decision to attack immediately. It was his only logical choice. The General was compelled to attack the village. If he had made no attempt to attack, the village would have escaped and split into numerous groups. He would then have been blamed for a ruined campaign. All of the officers in his command were in agreement since the goal of the expedition was to attack the Sioux and Cheyenne until they moved onto the reservations or were annihilated.

The greatest fear for Custer at this point was that the village would break up and flee in every direction leaving him holding the proverbial empty bag. This was a golden opportunity for the Seventh Cavalry to wrap up the entire campaign with one great battle. If General Custer succeeded, he would be the hero of the nation.

There was no longer time to scout the village or the surrounding terrain as the officers thought the village would surely attempt to flee from an entire regiment of cavalry. The column began moving in the direction of the Little Bighorn River. The pack train was placed under the command of Lieutenant Edward G. Mathey of Company M. One non-commissioned officer (NCO) and six privates from each of the twelve companies were also assigned to help care for the pack mules. The Arikara scout, Pretty

Face, was assigned to take care of the scouts' pack animals. In all, there were approximately 150 pack mules.[8]

Captain Thomas McDougall and his Company B were assigned as the rear guard for the day. Their duty was to protect the pack train from attack. Company B consisted of one officer and 41 men, after detaching one NCO and six enlisted men to the pack train. Captain McDougall's subaltern (second in command), Lieutenant Benjamin Hodgson, was assigned to Major Reno as his aide. The pack train and rear guard would wait twenty minutes before following the rest of the column.

By noon, the regiment had crossed the divide between the Rosebud and the Little Bighorn Valleys, which is approximately twelve miles from the Little Bighorn River. General Custer and his adjutant, Canadian born Lieutenant William W. Cooke, began to separate the regiment into four battalions. Major Marcus Reno (second in command) was assigned the command of a battalion of three companies. The approximately 130 man battalion consisted of Company A commanded by Captain Myles Moylan, Company G, commanded by Lieutenant Donald McIntosh, and Company M commanded by Captain Thomas French.

The senior captain, Frederick Benteen, was assigned a battalion consisting of his own Company H as well as Companies D and K. Company D commanded by Captain Thomas Weir and Company K by Lieutenant Edward S. Godfrey. Benteen's battalion consisted of approximately 125 officers and enlisted men.

Captain Benteen's battalion was soon sent to scout a line of bluffs approximately two miles away on the column's left front (a 45 degree left oblique). While Benteen's battalion was en route, Custer sent additional orders delivered by the Regimental Trumpeter, Henry Voss, and the Regimental Sergeant Major, William Sharrow.[9]

It is not known what General Custer's exact orders were as Captain Benteen was the lone survivor to hear them. Benteen never stated what his exact orders were. The gist of the orders was apparently for Benteen to scout the area to the south of the regiment's line of march, attack any hostile warriors he came across and inform General Custer immediately. He was to keep one officer and six enlisted men far enough ahead of his battalion to avoid any surprises. The two follow-up orders were for Captain

Benteen to continue on to the next line of bluffs and any after that. If he found nothing, he was to return to the trail.

Benteen's reconnaissance would allow Custer to know if there were other villages in the area that might surprise the column. It is also possible that General Custer was concerned that the Sioux would flee to the south. This decision by Custer would prove to be crucial to the outcome of the battle. Although Custer's reason for sending Captain Benteen's battalion to the left can be justified, the result was that Benteen's command would be too far out of position to participate in any of the afternoon's attacks.

As Benteen's battalion moved off to the left, the rest of the column continued along what is now known as Reno Creek toward the Little Bighorn River. Major Reno rode with his battalion on the left side of the dry creek while General Custer rode with the remaining five companies (C, E, F, I and L) on the right side. Custer split these five companies into two battalions.

One battalion commanded by Captain Myles Keogh consisted of three companies: his own Company I; Company L, commanded by Lieutenant James Calhoun; and Company C, commanded that day by Lieutenant Henry

M. Harrington. Captain Keogh's battalion consisted of approximately 125 officers and enlisted men. The remaining battalion was commanded by Captain George W. Yates. He was assigned his own Company F and Company E, commanded by Lieutenant Algernon E. Smith. The Yates' battalion consisted of approximately 76 officers and enlisted men. In addition to the five companies of the Keogh and Yates battalions, Custer was accompanied by the 10 or so officers and enlisted men assigned to Regimental Headquarters.

At about 2:15 p.m., the column reached the site of an abandoned tepee. It contained the remains of a dead warrior from the Rosebud battle that had occurred eight days earlier between General George Crook and many of the warriors that would soon be fighting the Seventh Cavalry. The Sioux often left their dead in abandoned lodges as a form of burial. The Cheyenne usually placed their dead on scaffolds or hid them in the mountains or on a river bank. The location of this tepee was approximately four miles east of the river. From this point, Custer ordered Major Reno to take the lead with his battalion.[10]

When the column reached a point about one and a quarter miles from the river, two of the Crow scouts observed two Sioux males from the village. The Crows managed to kill one of the Sioux, a boy named Deeds, but the other escaped northward in the direction of the village. Interpreter Fred Gerard claims that at this point he observed some other Sioux also running for the village and said to Custer, "Here are your Indians running like devils." General Custer then sent Lieutenant Cooke with instructions for Major Reno to charge those Indians at as fast a pace as he deemed prudent and that the whole outfit would support him.[11]

Some soldiers spoke of finding a great deal of cooking utensils and other camp equipment left behind at this point. They correctly assumed that the Indians had quickly abandoned this camp after learning of the approach of the regiment. This camp had contained very few Sioux, who had probably remained with the Sans Arc warrior who had been mortally wounded in the battle on Rosebud Creek eight days earlier. This warrior, believed to be the brother of Turning Bear, had succumbed to his wounds on June 24th.[12] These Sioux may also have been the ones observed by Fred Gerard.

Major Reno led his battalion out at a faster pace and soon reached the river. His battalion probably took about ten minutes to cross the river and reform on the west bank. Some soldiers took the time to water their thirsty horses while crossing. Lieutenants Varnum, Luther Hare and George Wallace crossed the river with most of the Indian scouts and their interpreters. They moved out ahead of Reno's battalion. Twenty-seven Indian scouts were assigned to Major Reno's battalion. They included nineteen Rees (including Bloody Knife), four Lakota (Sioux), two Pikunis (Robert and William Jackson) and two Crows (Half-Yellow Face and White Swan).[13]

Captain Keogh and Lieutenant Cooke also accompanied Reno as far as the river. During the crossing there were numerous sightings of the hostile warriors. Fred Gerard claimed that he had yet to cross the river when he saw that the warriors were coming out to meet Reno in force. He notified Lieutenant Cooke who assured Gerard that he would inform General Custer. Major Reno sent two separate couriers, Privates Archibald McIlhargey and John E. Mitchell, with the same basic message, "I have everything before me and they are strong." The approximate time was 3:00 p.m.[14]

[1] Fred Dustin, The Custer Tragedy, pp. 99

[2] Ibid, pp. 99-100

[3] Godfrey, pp. 19

[4] Dustin, pp. 100

[5] Ibid, pp. 101

[6] Marquis, Wooden Leg A Warrior Who Fought Custer, pp. 248-251, 269

[7] John S. Gray, Custer's Last Campaign, pp. 238

[8] Dustin, pp. 101-102

[9] John M. Carroll, The Benteen-Goldin Letters on Custer and His Last Battle, pp. 182-183

[10] Gray, Custer's Last Campaign, pp. 254

[11] Ibid, pp. 271-275

[12] Kenneth Hammer, Custer in 76, pp. 205

[13] Dustin, pp. 110

[14] Ibid, pp. 111

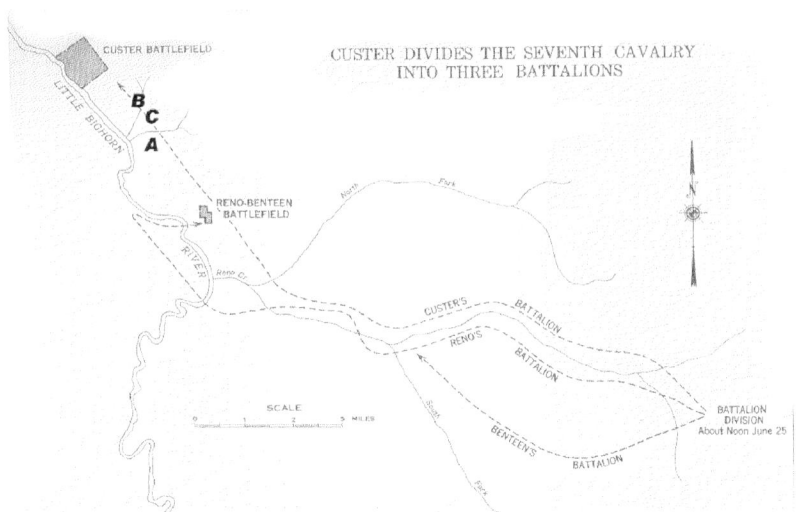

The basic movements of Custer's three battalions on June 25th. **A** is Medicine Tail Coulee. **B** is Deep Coulee. **C** is Nye-Cartwright Ridge.

Plains Indian burials. Dead warriors were often placed on scaffolds, inside of abandoned lodges, hidden on mountains or along the sides of river banks. Courtesy of James Dulemba.

III. The Valley Fight

After crossing the river, Reno's battalion formed up and began moving toward the village which was located about two miles to the north. As the valley opened up before them, Reno's battalion moved from column to line formation which was more effective when charging an enemy. Companies A and M formed a line in front while Company G formed a reserve line behind them. The order to charge was given.

When the village came into sight, the line extended to the left as Company G joined the line on the right flank. The charging soldiers rode through a prairie dog village as they passed a stand of timber on their right flank. The battalion continued to charge in this formation until it reached a point approximately nine hundred yards from the village.

At this point, Major Reno made the decision to halt the charge and dismount to fight on foot. This decision was made because Reno had seen a shallow coulee or watercourse ahead of them.[1] This claim was supported by Lieutenant Charles DeRudio of Company A, Captain

Moylan and Lieutenant Hare, who said that the warriors came pouring out of the coulee as if they had been waiting to surprise the battalion.[2]

At the southern end of the large encampment, the village was in chaos. The non-combatants were busy trying to run away to the north and west while the warriors were moving to stop the advancing soldiers. Sitting Bull and some of the other Hunkpapa leaders managed to lessen the panic and urged more warriors to face the attacking soldiers. Sitting Bull and the others provided the necessary morale boost that most villages lacked in similar situations. They stopped panicking and began fighting.[3]

Three soldiers, Privates George E. Smith, J. H. Meyer and Roman Rutten, were unable to control their horses which ran away with them heading toward the village. This occurred at the halt. Meyer and Rutten were both able to regain control of their mounts and returned to their lines with only wounds, but Smith's horse carried him into the village where he was killed.[4] Another account has Private George E. Smith being killed at the edge of the timber.[5] This shows how confusing eyewitness accounts can be.

As the battalion dismounted, every fourth man became a horse holder for three other soldiers. This allowed the other three men to fire their rifles without their horses disturbing their aim. The horse holders were ordered to the rear and later into a timbered area near the river under the command of Lieutenant Luther Hare. The battalion's fighting strength was reduced to about ninety-five men. This number did not include scouts and interpreters who were not expected to serve on the firing line (most didn't).

The skirmish line was about two hundred fifty yards in length. The Indian scouts made an attempt to run off part of the Sioux pony herd but were unable to capture many. An Arikara scout, Bob-Tailed Bull, was killed on the extreme left of the skirmish line. He would be the battalion's second casualty of the battle.

The line advanced about one hundred yards closer to the village where the firing became a little more intense. First Sergeant John Ryan of Company M led some troopers to secure some nearby lodges that had already been abandoned by their owners. These lodges were set up near the river, about eight hundred yards from the Hunkpapa camp circle.

The warriors began to ride around the right flank of the skirmish line threatening the horse holders. Reno removed Company G from the line and placed them in the timbered area near the river to protect the horses and their holders. The soldiers were spread out to make up for the reduction of men on the line. Now the skirmish line consisted of about seventy men. It is estimated that about five hundred warriors were then facing Reno's battalion.[6] A large group of these warriors then began to ride around the left flank of Reno's line causing the officers to move the line to the edge of the timber and reface it outward.

At this point, we have only about three dead on the soldiers' side. Private G. E. Smith, whose runaway horse carried him into the village and Bob-Tailed Bull, killed on the far left flank. The third was Sergeant Miles O'Hara of Company M who was mortally wounded in the chest while still on the firing line.

The soldiers had only been firing for about twenty minutes, but most had used up all of the ammunition that they carried and had gotten more from their saddlebags. Each soldier had been issued one hundred rounds of ammunition for his carbine and twenty-four rounds for his pistol. The pistol ammunition and about half of the carbine ammunition was kept in their cartridge cases and pockets while the remaining carbine ammunition was kept in their saddle bags.

The firing line was roughly in a bow-shape facing primarily west. Reno's situation was quickly turning into a desperate one. His small battalion was no longer on the offensive, but was pinned down in the timber which was an area that encompassed about ten acres. Their backs were now to the river. The battalion's supply of ammunition was being quickly depleted and the realization set in that the enemy was growing stronger and more aggressive by the minute. Reno's men were outnumbered by more than five to one. General Custer's promised support had failed to materialize.

The warriors encircled the timber and increased their rate of fire at the soldiers defending it. Private George Lorentz of Company M was shot in the stomach. Privates William E. Morris and Frank Neely attempted to help him but he was in too much pain to allow himself to be touched. He would be left behind during the upcoming retreat.[7]

Major Reno consulted with Captain Moylan then made his decision. He would form up the battalion and charge through the warriors so that he could cross back to the east side of the river and rally on the bluffs. He issued his orders to the company commanders personally and through his adjutant, Lieutenant Hodgson. The companies were formed in columns of four in a small glade within the timber.

While the battalion was still reorganizing, the hostile warriors took advantage of the situation and increased their infiltration of the timber area. A small number of enemy warriors fired a volley killing one soldier and the Arikara scout Bloody Knife. Bloody Knife's brains and blood were splattered over Major Reno, who was nearby.[8]

Major Reno decided to wait no longer and led the charge out of the timber. The warriors were temporarily confused by this action which allowed the battalion to quickly break through toward the river. However, the warriors soon recovered and began following the soldiers, pulling the slower men off their horses. Private David Summers was killed as Company M emerged from the timber.[9]

Company G was slow getting to their horses as word of the order to mount up was late getting to them. Private John Rapp, Lieutenant McIntosh's orderly, was killed while holding their horses in the timber. Soldiers were taking the first horse they found and left the timber in a hurry. Private John Lattman took McIntosh's unattended horse.[10]

Lieutenant McIntosh was forced to borrow a horse, and unfortunately, received one whose picket pin was dragging from its rope between the horse's legs. He could not get the horse to turn in the direction of the river, causing him to be easily singled out by a number of warriors who surrounded him. Private William Morris observed Lieutenant McIntosh with his gun in his hand, shooting at the warriors that eventually killed him.[11]

Farrier Benjamin J. Wells of Company G lost control of his horse which bolted into the hostile Indians during the retreat. Private James P. Boyle of Company G stated that Wells' body was found in the river north or northwest of where Lieutenant McIntosh lay. The Sioux women had evidently not found him because his clothes were still on his body.[12]

The movement to cross the river quickly became a panicked rout, the soldiers behaving like a disorganized mob. At least it was in the rear of the column. Things got worse as the soldiers jumped their mounts into the river and crossed, only to find that the trail leading to the top of the bluffs was steep and of single file width. This caused a traffic jam of sorts which not only increased the confusion and panic but also allowed the warriors more time to kill those soldiers on the flanks and rear of the column.

Dr. James M. DeWolf chose to climb another trail leading up and to the left. He would be killed near the top by warriors who had gotten there first. Lieutenant Varnum had started to follow him but was called back by soldiers who had seen the warriors.[13] Privates William D. Meyer and Henry Gordon of Company M were killed while climbing the bluffs by warriors on the east side of the river. Some warriors were also reportedly on the bluffs south of the line of retreat.[14]

Lieutenant Hodgson was wounded during the crossing and lost his horse. He was pulled across the river by an enlisted man who gave him a stirrup to hold on to. Unfortunately, the Lieutenant was killed immediately upon reaching the east bank of the river. His friends claimed that he had told them a few days earlier of his intention to grab onto someone's stirrup if that very circumstance ever occurred.[15]

As the men reached the top of the bluffs, they had to be reorganized. Some of the officers attempted to form them into a perimeter while others tried to set up some cover fire for those soldiers still crossing the river. Little cover fire was ever given. One soldier, Private John W. Wallace of Company G, showed his courage during the retreat. He killed one of the warriors and took his scalp.[16]

By the time this hasty maneuver was completed, Reno's battalion had sustained numerous losses. Three officers, including Dr. DeWolf, were killed and one was reported missing (Lieutenant Charles DeRudio). There were also twenty-nine enlisted men killed, seven wounded, and more than a dozen others missing. Sioux interpreter Isaiah Dorman and scout Charley Reynolds were killed as well. Arikaras Bloody Knife and Bob-Tail Bull were also killed. One Crow scout, White Swan, was wounded and another Arikara scout killed. Only about seventy-five soldiers with Reno were still capable of defending themselves.

Isaiah Dorman had the unique distinction of being the only black man to serve with Custer's forces. He was highly respected by most of the soldiers in an era when racism was an acceptable practice. He must have been a remarkable man to have earned their respect. He was married to a Sioux woman and was known to many of the Sioux, including Sitting Bull. They considered him a traitor for his participation in the attack on the village and mutilated his body severely for it.[17]

Some would call Reno's withdrawal a mistake, but anyone who did not participate in that part of the battle could not know for sure whether it was the right or wrong choice. The men who could best judge the situation as it was would have been Reno and his officers. They saw more than most of the enlisted men and had more of an opportunity to see what was developing across the entire line.

A withdrawal was necessary for the survival of Reno's battalion; however, it could have been handled in a more orderly fashion and with fewer casualties. He could possibly have held the position for another ten or twenty minutes before being forced to withdraw. He undoubtedly felt that within a few more minutes his battalion would have been unable to escape. Almost all of Reno's officers supported his actions in the valley that day. Only Captain Thomas French criticized Reno's retreat from the timber.[18]

Reno would always claim that it was not a retreat but a charge. Technically he was correct because he had to charge through the warriors in order to withdraw to the bluffs on the east side of the river. Those soldiers in the rear of the formation would probably have viewed the movement as a retreat as they did not have to break through the warriors. They were actually being chased by warriors all the way to the river. The difference in opinion was a result of their individual positions during the movement.

---

[1] W. A. Graham, The Reno Court of Inquiry, pp. 213

[2] Hammer, Custer in 76, pp. 66

[3] Richard G. Hardorff, Lakota Recollections of the Custer Fight, pp. 109

[4] Dustin, pp. 111

[5] Hammer, pp. 131

[6] Graham, The Reno Court of Inquiry, pp. 90

[7] Hammer, pp. 131

[8] Ronald H. Nichols, In Custer's Shadow, pp. 180

[9] Hammer, pp. 131

[10] Walter M. Camp, Custer & Company, pp. 77-78

[11] Ibid, pp. 132

[12] Nichols, Men With Custer, pp. 353

[13] Graham, The Reno Court of Inquiry, pp. 54

[14] Hammer, pp. 131

[15] Graham, The Custer Myth, pp. 140

[16] Ibid, pp. 141

[17] Hardorff, Lakota Recollections of the Custer Fight, pp. 101-102

[18] Robert M. Utley, Custer and the Great Controversy, pp. 106

Major Marcus Reno, commanded a battalion at the Little Bighorn. He would be accused of cowardice by General Custer's friends and supporters in the years following the battle. Courtesy of LBHBNM.

General Custer posing with his trophy grizzly bear killed during the 1874 Black Hills Expedition. On the far left is Arikara scout Bloody Knife, who was killed at the Little Bighorn. Courtesy of Library of Congress.

Left: Lieutenant Charles Varnum was General Custer's Chief of Scouts. Right: Lieutenant Luther R. Hare of Company K. Courtesy of LBHBNM.

Left: Lieutenant George D. Wallace of Company G. He was killed at Wounded Knee in 1890. Right: Lieutenant Charles C. DeRudio of Company A hid in the timber with Private Tomas O'Neil after Reno's retreat from the valley. Pictures courtesy of LBHBNM.

Reno's battalion moves into line as it rides down the valley. Company G moves forward and is added to the right flank of the line as the valley becomes wider.

As the warriors turn their flank, Companies A and M were forced to retreat into the timber with Company G and the horse holders.

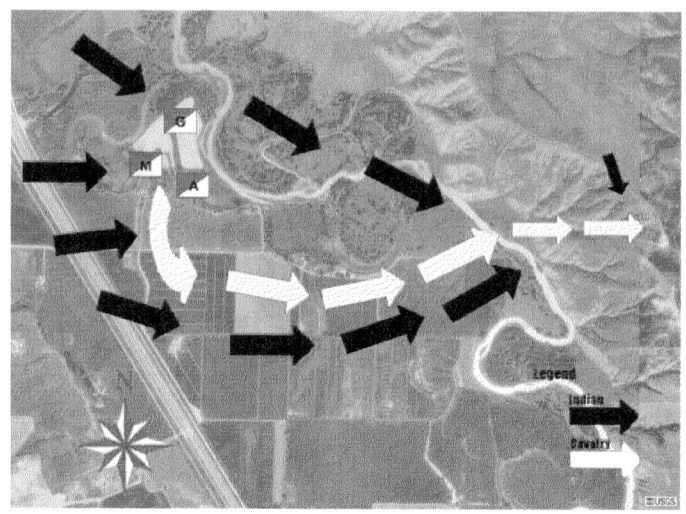

Reno's battalion retreats from the timber to the bluffs across the river. The warriors quickly give chase and kill those who become separated.

Lieutenant Benjamin H. Hodgson served as Major Reno's adjutant during the fight in the valley. He was killed after being pulled across the river. Courtesy of James Dulemba.

Charles A. Reynolds, "Lonesome Charley", was killed during Reno's retreat from the valley. Courtesy of James Dulemba.

Left: Captain Thomas H. French commanded Company M. He was critical of Reno's retreat order.
Center: Lieutenant Donald McIntosh commanded Company G was killed during the retreat from the valley.
Right: Captain Myles Moylan commanded Company A. Like Reno, he was disliked by most of the other officers.
Courtesy of LBHBNM.

IV. Custer Moves North

It is uncertain when Custer made his decision not to follow Reno across the river. Was it before or after receiving the three messages about the warriors coming out of the village to meet Reno's attack? It is known that General Custer and his five companies watered their horses along the North Fork of Reno Creek, about three quarters of a mile from the river. Sergeant Daniel Kanipe of Company C claimed that the appearance of sixty or seventy warriors on the bluffs to the north convinced General Custer to turn his five remaining companies in that direction.[1] Sergeant Kanipe's claim was supported by Standing Bear, one of the Sioux warriors on the bluffs.[2]

Custer certainly wasn't worried about rounding up every stray warrior in the area. It wasn't possible with the number of men he had available. However, he wouldn't have wanted them on his flank or in the rear of his attacking forces, especially if he didn't know how many more were behind them.

Another possibility regarding Custer's decision not to cross the river was that the messages from Reno prompted the General to change direction. The messages from Reno would have confirmed the typical Indian tactics in Custer's mind. Reno's battalion may then have become the bait intended to draw out the warriors while Custer went after the non-combatants. He could then have used them as hostages to force the warriors to surrender. General Custer might then have ended the battle with fewer losses in men. Unfortunately, Major Reno was not informed of this new plan of attack.

Somewhere between the North Fork of Reno Creek and the bluffs that Major Reno's battalion would later retreat to, the horses of at least three soldiers gave out. Privates John Brennan, Peter Thompson and James Watson could no longer keep up with the column. These three soldiers all belonged to Company C. Brennan would turn around and join the pack train. Thompson and Watson apparently attempted to follow their company on foot until confronted by hostile warriors. They would spend the next few hours hiding in ravines along the bluffs. They were observed by the Arikara scout named Soldier who confirmed that their horses were too exhausted to continue.[3]

General Custer sent his four remaining Crow scouts ahead with Mitch Boyer and followed them to the north. While on high ground overlooking the valley, Custer was observed by some of Reno's command.[4] General Custer may have been observed again near Sharpshooter's Ridge prior to turning down into Cedar Coulee.

Mitch Boyer and the four Crow scouts went to Weir Point and farther north utilizing the higher terrain. They would observe

Reno's fight and subsequent retreat as well as the commencement of Custer's fight. Only Mitch Boyer and the young scout, Curly would rejoin Custer. It may even have been Mitch Boyer and the Crow scouts that were observed by Reno's men when they believed they had seen General Custer on the bluffs.

As General Custer reached the junction of Cedar and Medicine Tail Coulees, Captain Tom Custer sent Sergeant Kanipe of Company C back to hasten the pack train. Sergeant Kanipe was to direct them to ignore the trail and travel straight across country instead. If he came across Captain Benteen, he was to hurry him as well.[5]

About ten or fifteen minutes later, General Custer sent Trumpeter John D. Martin (Giovanni Martini), a recent Italian immigrant, back to find Captain Benteen. He was instructed to tell him to come quickly. Lieutenant Cooke gave Martin a written message for Benteen, "Benteen. Come on. Big village. Be quick. Bring packs. P.S. Bring packs. W. W. Cooke."[6] Martin stated positively that his departure from Custer took place about 600 yards from Medicine Tail Ford.[7]

Martin would follow the column's trail back to Reno Creek and Captain Benteen. He stated that he heard firing from Custer's direction as he reached the top of the hill and saw General Custer retreating towards Calhoun Hill.[8] He also stated that he observed warriors riding around waving blankets. Indians would often wave blankets to scare the soldiers' horses.[9]

While he could have heard the beginning of the skirmish in Medicine Tail Coulee, he was undoubtedly incorrect about which ridge Custer was moving toward. It was far too soon for the movement to Calhoun Hill. Martin's own mount would be wounded about this time. Boston Custer would allegedly mention the horse's wound to Martin as he passed and asked for directions to the General.[10]

Before we can continue, we must update ourselves on the simultaneous movements of two other battalions: Benteen's and the pack train/rear guard. This should be done here because, as we shall see, Boston Custer left the pack train to join his brothers and is seen by all but Reno's column. Boston was George and Tom Custer's younger brother. He also talked with Martin and had been observed by Sergeant Kanipe.

---

[1] Hammer, pp. 97

[2] Ibid, pp. 215

[3] Orin G. Libby, The Arikara Narrative of Custer's Campaign and the Battle of the Little Bighorn, pp. 116

[4] Graham, The Reno Court of Inquiry, pp. 114-115

[5] Hammer, pp. 92-95

[6] Lloyd J. Overfield II, The Little Big Horn, 1876 The Official Communications, Documents and Reports, pp. 40

[7] Ibid, pp. 105

[8] Hammer, pp. 101

[9] Hammer, pp. 103-104

[10] Ibid, pp. 101

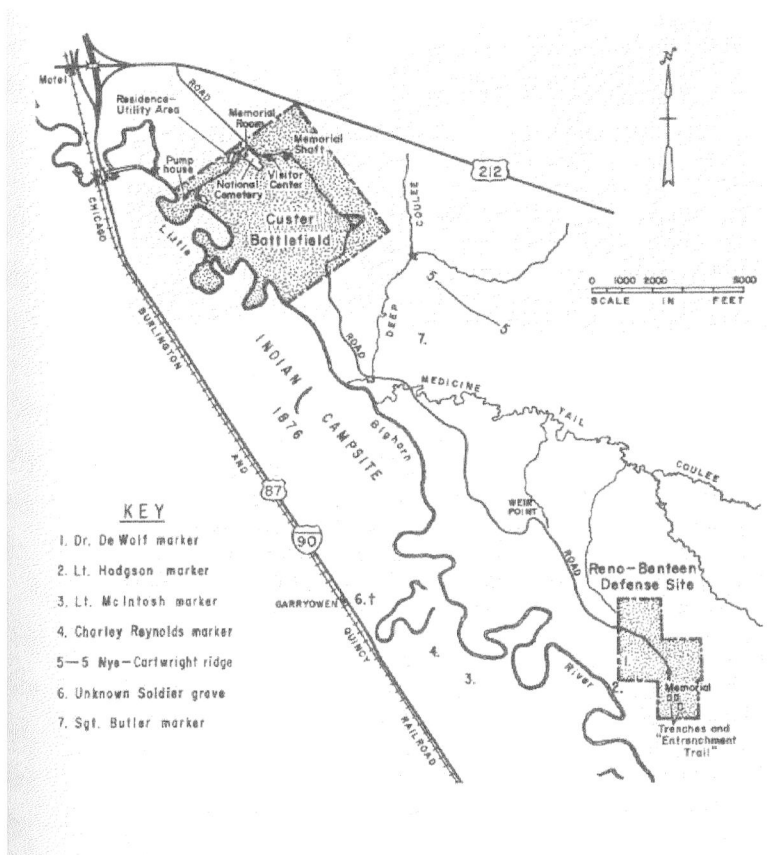

Map of Little Bighorn Battlefield. Courtesy of the Little Bighorn Battlefield National Monument.

Left: Trumpeter John Martin carried Custer's last message. His poor grasp of the English language made him a poor choice for a messenger.
Right: Sergeant Daniel A. Kanipe of Company C. The order he delivered for the pack train to move straight to Custer was apparently ignored or misunderstood. Courtesy of LBHBNM.

V. Benteen and the Pack Train

We must bear in mind that many activities were occurring at the same time. While General Custer was busy sending Major Reno's battalion to attack the village, Captain Benteen's battalion was just completing their scout of the area to the left (south) of Reno Creek. It did not take Captain Benteen long to realize that there was not much likelihood of any village camping along the path he was sent to scout. Nevertheless, it was his duty to verify that very point.

If there had been warriors along his path, they might flank the main column or attack the pack train. Due to the uneven terrain, Captain Benteen had to be thorough. He could not just ride along at a brisk trot as that would have invited ambush and worn out his battalion's horses. Neither of these options would have been appealing to any officer. Benteen had to stop at three different lines of low bluffs. He sent Lieutenant Francis Gibson and five enlisted men to the top of each set of bluffs to look for any signs of hostile warriors. To avoid possible ambush by Sioux warriors, Captain Benteen had to wait for Lieutenant Gibson's signal before he led the battalion to the next line of bluffs.

After about five miles of this triangular-shaped detour, Benteen knew that the area to the south contained no hostile Indians. Realizing that he might be needed elsewhere, Benteen chose to rejoin the rest of the regiment. The point where Benteen rejoined the trail along Reno Creek was near a morass or marsh, about a mile east of the lodge containing the dead warrior. Captain Benteen took advantage of the morass to water his horses for about ten or more minutes before continuing along the trail. His horses had not been watered for almost twenty-four hours and were extremely thirsty. Even with his detour, Benteen rejoined the trail about a mile ahead of the much slower pack train.

About the time Benteen was watering his horses, Boston Custer passed the battalion in search of his older brothers, George and Tom.[1] Boston had been hired as a quartermaster scout and was assigned to the pack train. He was apparently in a great hurry to join his brothers and his nephew, eighteen year old Autie Reed, for the battle. There was a strong family bond between the relatives.

Now, many people might argue that since Boston Custer was able to reach his brothers that Benteen could have made it as well. This sounds logical, at first, but only if we forget a few important details. Boston Custer's mount was still fresh at the time. When Benteen returned to the trail, he is still about five miles behind General Custer who had already turned north. Although Benteen's battalion only traveled about two miles farther than the other battalions because of his detour, the terrain was much rougher. He also needed to water his horses which Reno and Custer had already done. He was not yet in a hurry, as he had heard no shooting and had received no further orders.

Boston Custer also had no real responsibilities to keep him from traveling where he wished, so he was able to maintain a pace of his own choosing. Captain Benteen was responsible for the condition of his battalion's horses and needed to keep them as fresh as possible for whatever fighting that might occur. Boston galloped away and was soon out of sight. He would pass Sergeant Kanipe and Trumpeter Martin along the way. Martin, as you will remember, was carrying Custer's last known message.

Just after Benteen's battalion left the morass, the front of the pack train arrived and proceeded to get bogged down. The mules were nearly mad with thirst. They had gone without water for twenty-four hours as well and were forced to carry the heavy burdens of food and ammunition crates. It is uncertain whether the mules refused to leave the morass out of exhaustion or because they were mired in mud. Benteen would come to the burial lodge after about fifteen minutes and would stop shortly to investigate the now smoldering lodge. Either the soldiers of General Custer's column or the scouts had attempted to burn it down. The scouts would later blame the soldiers for destroying the lodge. The soldiers blamed the scouts so we can't be certain who really destroyed the tepee.

About a mile after he left the lone tepee, Benteen encountered Sergeant Kanipe who had been sent by Captain Thomas Custer to hurry the pack train to General Custer's location. Sergeant Kanipe gave the message to Captain Benteen who informed him that he was not in charge of the pack train and directed him to Captain McDougall. As the sergeant rode back towards the pack train, he yelled out to the men of Benteen's battalion, "We've got them, boys!"[2] For some unexplained reason the pack train continued along Reno Creek following the trail everyone else took and made no effort to ride straight across country to Custer's five companies.

Sergeant Kanipe may not have informed Captain McDougall or Lieutenant Mathey of the order to cut across country. If Sergeant Kanipe had given one of the two officers the message, it would seem likely that they would have had him lead them straight to General Custer instead of letting him fall in with his friends who were assigned to the pack train. Neither of the officers knew where to go. Only Kanipe knew the location of Custer's two battalions at that time. It seems possible that Sergeant Kanipe failed to inform either of them that they were to move straight to General Custer instead of following the trail.

The message delivered by Sergeant Kanipe did cause Benteen to increase his speed. Within fifteen minutes after his meeting with Kanipe, Benteen received a second message delivered by Martin with the written orders mentioned earlier. Since the orders were contradictory, hurry up and bring the packs, Benteen required more information. He needed to know whether Custer needed more men fast or required ammunition. He could not hurry and bring the pack train with him as it was too slow.

Captain Benteen asked Martin about the Indians and was told they were "skedaddling."[3] This, combined with Kanipe's "We've got them, boys!", would have given Benteen the impression that General Custer had the Sioux and Cheyenne on the run and simply needed more men and ammunition for the mop up of the village. As Kanipe had already been sent back to the pack train to hurry it along, Benteen could see no logic to sending another courier with the same orders.

Captain Benteen picked up his pace until he reached a point overlooking the river above Reno's original crossing point. Benteen could hear shooting and observed the end of Reno's retreat to the bluffs. Seeing that the tail of Reno's column was being overwhelmed by hundreds of warriors must have been very confusing to Benteen as he was not aware of the detachment of Major Reno's battalion or their orders. If Custer had the Indians on the run, then what was going on in front of him?

Benteen's attention was quickly called to the presence of Indians on the high ground to the north. It turned out to be the Crow scouts Goes Ahead, White Man Runs Him and Hairy Moccasin who had separated from Mitch Boyer,

Curly and Custer's two battalions. The scouts waved for Benteen to come up the hill. They then directed Benteen's battalion to Reno's location on the bluffs.

Benteen joined Major Reno on the bluffs at approximately 4:10 p.m. The remnants of Reno's battalion had been placed in a crude perimeter on the bluffs, but they were not in good condition. Major Reno, as well as the other surviving officers of his battalion, seemed to be quite shaken from their disastrous retreat from the valley. Reno's demeanor was described as "greatly excited" by Lieutenant Winfield Scott Edgerly of Company D.[4] It is quite likely that most of the officers and enlisted men were also greatly excited after their hair raising withdrawal from the valley.

Captain Benteen asked Major Reno about General Custer's location. Reno pointed off to the north, indicating where he thought Custer was located from the tracks of the Custer command's horses. Benteen showed Major Reno his orders which Reno read and returned to him. He then pleaded with Captain Benteen to stop and wait while he got his men reorganized. This would allow them to both link up with Custer.[5] Benteen agreed as he now knew he must wait on the pack train after all and that the bluffs were as good a place as any to wait.

At about 4:20 p.m. Lieutenant Hare was sent to hurry the pack train along. Lieutenant Hare borrowed Lieutenant Godfrey's horse as his own had been wounded. Upon reaching the pack train he delivered the order to hurry up and to cut out the ammunition packs as soon as possible and to send them forward.[6] Reno's men averaged only about forty cartridges apiece at that time. Undoubtedly, many men would have had more than five cartridges if they had been more conservative with their ammunition on the firing line. The horse holders also had most of their ammunition as they had not been on the line. The men that lost their horses during the retreat to the bluffs also lost most of their extra ammunition which was kept in their saddlebags.

Lieutenant Hare met the pack train about one mile from Reno's position and returned with the ammunition mule after about twenty minutes.[7] It would be another few minutes before the pack train arrived on the bluffs. Captain McDougall had placed one platoon from Company B in front of the pack train and the other in the rear.[8]

Many have been critical of Major Reno for not immediately riding to General Custer's aid, and the same is true of Captain Benteen's stopping to help Major Reno. However, Major Reno's battalion was in no condition to ride to Custer as many were now without horses, and most of the wounded could not ride. They were also low on ammunition which would have made them incapable of sustained combat.

Captain Benteen could have ignored Major Reno's request for help, but what would have been the point? He had the same amount of men as Reno before his fight. He also had become responsible for the pack train after receiving the message delivered by Martin and it was obvious that Reno's men couldn't protect themselves much less the pack train. The proximity of the warriors would allow them to get between Benteen and the pack train if he continued toward Custer without it. Another crucial factor was that due to the dead, wounded and missing, General Custer had approximately the same number of men with him as Benteen and Reno had combined. The general feeling was that he was as capable of taking care of himself as they were.

[1] Gray, Custer's Last Campaign, pp. 258

[2] Graham, The Reno Court of Inquiry, pp.176

[3] Ibid, pp. 138

[4] Graham, The Custer Myth, pp. 317

[5] Hammer, pp. 101, 105

[6] Nichols, Reno Court of Inquiry, pp. 289

[7] Hammer, pp. 66

[8] Hammer, pp. 70

Captain Frederick W. Benteen, commanded a battalion at the Little Bighorn. His hatred for General Custer did not diminish even after Custer's death. Courtesy of LBHBNM

Captain Thomas McDougall (left) commanded Company B which was assigned as the rear guard during the battle. Lieutenant Edward G. Mathey (right) of Company M commanded the pack train. Courtesy of James Dulemba and LBHBNM.

Four of Custer's Crow scouts. From left to right: White Man Runs Him, Hairy Moccasin, Curly and Goes Ahead. The photograph was taken on Custer Hill in 1913 by Rodman Wanamaker. Courtesy of LBHBNM.

VI. Medicine Tail Coulee

We pick up with General Custer's five companies where we left them in Medicine Tail Coulee. Mitch Boyer and Curly watched the activity in the village and Reno's valley fight from Weir Ridge. From this point forward, we have very little certain knowledge of Custer's actions. In this chapter, we shall try to unravel some of the confusion of Custer's movements. To do so we will mix archeological evidence, eyewitness testimony and speculation.

Custer may have sent out another courier from Company C at the junction of Medicine Tail and Cedar Coulees. This one was allegedly sent to the north, likely in an effort to find General Terry and hurry him if possible. The body of a soldier from Company C, and believed to have been Private Nathan Short, was discovered a month later near the Rosebud. His dead horse and his weapons were found with him indicating that he had been wounded and escaped to that point.[1]

It is more likely that this soldier was an escapee from a later point in the battle, or a deserter, rather than a courier. The reason for this hypothesis is that General Custer could not have been aware of his predicament at that point in the battle. He would also have informed any courier that General Terry could be found somewhere along the Bighorn River, not Rosebud Creek.

He may have been wounded by Little Wolf's warriors, who had been following the Seventh Cavalry for the past few days in search of the larger Indian encampment. After the shooting incident over the crate of hard tack that morning, they had detoured north before moving west to the Little Bighorn River. Little Wolf's small village did not arrive at the large encampment until after the Custer portion of the fight was over.[2]

After Custer entered Medicine Tail Coulee and turned northwest toward the ford, several things began to happen. First, Custer's five companies split into two battalions commanded by Captains Keogh and Yates. Second, Boston Custer arrived with news that Benteen was on the trail once again and that he had passed the two couriers. Third, Custer moved toward Medicine Tail Ford with Captain Yates' battalion until he was met by Mitch Boyer and Curly who had descended Weir Ridge. Fourth, Boyer informed General Custer that Major Reno's battalion was in full retreat, although they had probably only retreated into the timber at that time.³

As the Yates battalion reached Nye-Cartwright Ridge, they came under fire from a small group of Sioux and Cheyenne warriors. Yates' battalion dismounted and took up positions along the ridge. From the cartridge casings found in the area it would appear that the soldiers fired almost five hundred rounds at the warriors defending Medicine Tail Ford.⁴ Although the fighting was brisk initially, no serious attempt was made by Captain Yates to cross the river at this location.

Keogh's battalion did not move toward the ford with Yates' battalion because they stayed back to engage the sixty or seventy warriors General Custer had followed from the North Fork of Reno Creek. These warriors had not retreated toward the ford after reaching Medicine Tail Coulee. If they had turned toward the ford, Captain Yates would have been met there by more than twenty warriors.

The warriors facing Keogh's battalion split into two groups: one on each side of Luce Ridge.⁵ One group stayed to the north of the two battalions. These warriors reached Calhoun Hill and Calhoun Ridge (also known as Finley

Ridge) prior to the Yates and Keogh battalions. General Custer's two battalions were then caught between warriors coming from at least three directions as a small group of warriors from the south began to arrive. Captain Keogh soon led his battalion to Calhoun Hill to drive away the warriors who had moved there from Medicine Tail Coulee.[6]

It seems likely that Captain Keogh ordered Company C to take up a position on Calhoun Ridge in order to protect the right flank of Yates' battalion and later to cover its withdrawal to Calhoun Hill. The few warriors on the ridge would have retreated as Company C charged towards them.

Lieutenant Harrington, the acting commander for C Company, set up his skirmish line along Calhoun Ridge. His line extended from Greasy Grass Ridge toward Calhoun Hill. Their skirmish line was formed facing generally south and west.

With more warriors arriving steadily to reinforce those defending the ford, Yates' battalion retreated to Calhoun Hill. The warriors soon followed the Yates battalion during their withdrawal from the Nye-Cartwright Ridge. The first attacks against Company C began quickly after.

On Calhoun Hill, Custer's brother-in-law, Lieutenant James Calhoun, had Company L dismount. James Calhoun was married to General Custer's sister, Margaret. He placed the men in a skirmish line on the hill later named for him and their horses were taken to a ravine located to the north of Calhoun Hill and east of Battle Ridge. This ravine would become known as Horse Holder's Ravine. At this point, the warriors were confined primarily to the areas around Medicine Tail Coulee and Deep Coulee; however, they were receiving reinforcements by the minute from the village as well as from the southern bluffs.

While Companies C and L were holding back the warriors, General Custer conducted an officers' call behind Calhoun Hill.[7] During this meeting, Custer decided to move toward the northwest with Companies E and F in hopes of capturing some of the fleeing non-combatants. Keogh's battalion was assigned to defend their current positions while awaiting reinforcement by Captain Benteen's battalion. They were probably supposed to distract the warriors from the movements of Yates' battalion as well.

General Custer was apparently unaware that the momentum had changed in favor of the warriors who were now on the offensive. This episode ends with Custer riding to the northwest with Companies E and F, as well as his headquarters staff. His staff was comprised of his brother, Captain Tom Custer, a two time Congressional Medal of Honor recipient, his adjutant, Lieutenant Cooke, Assistant Surgeon George E. Lord, Sergeant Major Sharrow, Chief Trumpeter Henry Voss, Trumpeter Henry C. Dose, Colors Sergeants Robert H. Hughes and John Vickory. Three civilians were also riding with this group: Boston Custer, Harry Armstrong (Autie) Reed, and Mark Kellogg (a reporter).

By splitting his forces again, Custer was compounding his previous mistakes. He had continuously split his already greatly inferior force until each piece was too small to take care of itself. He then continued to move farther away from the battalions that he presumably expected to support him. If you think you need help, it would seem more logical to move in the direction that the help is expected to come from rather than away from it. Since he did the opposite, we must conclude that he was unaware of his predicament. This decision to split his force again would remove any chance that the Yates and Keogh battalions had of surviving.

[1] Hammer, pp. 126, 137, 146, 248

[2] Marquis, <u>Wooden Leg A Warrior Who Fought Custer</u>, pp. 269

[3] Ibid, pp. 166-167, 172,

[4] Gregory F. Michno, <u>Lakota Noon</u>, pp. 153

[5] Ibid, pp. 136-137

[6] Hardorff, <u>Lakota Recollections of the Custer Fight</u>, pp. 143

[7] Hammer, pp. 158

Left: Curly, the young Crow scout was the last survivor to see Custer alive. Right: Mitch Boyer, noted Frontier scout, killed with the soldiers of Captain Yates' battalion. Courtesy of James Dulemba.

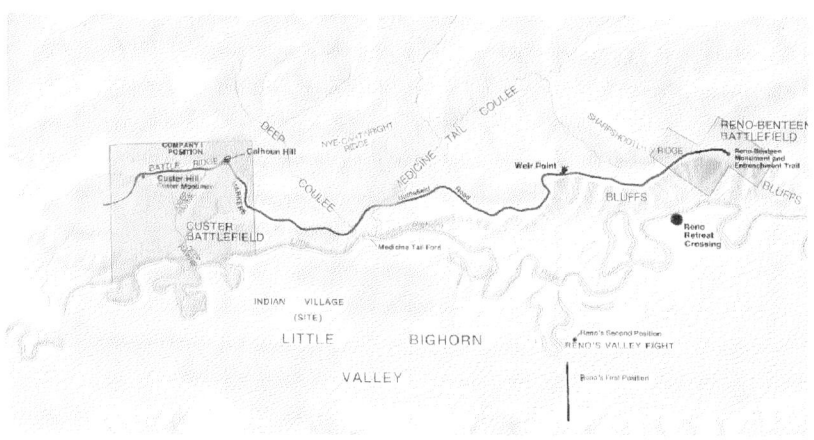

Another view of the Little Bighorn Battlefield. The distance from Calhoun Hill to the Reno-Benteen Battlefield is approximately 4 miles. Nye-Cartwright Ridge is located between Deep Coulee and Medicine Tail Coulee. The Custer fight would begin there. Map adapted from National Park Service map.

VII. The Keogh Fight

As the Keogh fight began Company L's horse holders led their company's horses into a shallow ravine to the north for protection. This ravine was on the east side of Battle Ridge as stated earlier. Company L's skirmish line was formed facing south toward Deep Coulee. Company C's horse holders led their horses behind the ridge that they were defending. This was most likely in Calhoun Coulee. Company C's skirmish line was still facing south and west.

Some men were assigned to protect their right (west) flank on Greasy Grass Ridge. Only seven bodies were found on Greasy Grass Ridge which leaves us with the assumption that only two squads (four men per squad) were assigned to protect the company's right flank.[1] Captain Keogh placed his own Company I in reserve along Battle Ridge.

Two Eagles and others stated that some of the soldiers were dismounted while others remained mounted at both of those locations. Two Eagles believed that many of the soldiers had abandoned or lost their horses. The officers and possibly some non-commissioned officers would have remained mounted to better direct the firing of the skirmish lines. Remaining visible to the men also provided a degree of moral support in desperate situations.[2]

As Custer moved to the northwest, Keogh's battalion was still in good condition, lightly skirmishing with the warriors. However, several hundred yards away, the warriors were crossing the river in ever increasing numbers as they were no longer concerned with Major Reno's beaten battalion. They began to pass around Company L's left (east) flank, taking up positions on the higher ridges overlooking Calhoun's horse holders. Other warriors turned left (north) immediately after crossing the river and took up positions at the western base of Greasy Grass Ridge.

The warriors on the ridges to the east of Calhoun Hill began to harass the Company L horses and holders. They eventually began to infiltrate down into the ravine area around the horses and started to stampede them. The holders could not fire accurately and hold their horses at the same time. Captain Keogh was then forced to use his reserve company to protect Calhoun's horses whose saddle bags contained half of Company L's ammunition. This provides us with a credible reason for Keogh moving into the depression northeast of Battle Ridge.

Captain Keogh was an experienced officer who had more sense than to choose a defensive position in a depression with higher ridges on three sides. Likewise, he would not have placed himself and Company I in reserve at this location. He would not have been able to see how his other two companies were faring and the warriors on the ridges to the east would have quickly made the position a poor position to be in. The area was only suitable as a reserve position if the soldiers controlled the surrounding ridges. Additionally, there has been no archeological evidence to indicate that Company I retreated into the depression from Battle Ridge.

The only logical reason left for moving into that depression was to attack. His men were found in a sort of line paralleling Battle Ridge. Some of them were obviously attempting to retreat, but that alone would not explain the linear groups nearest to Keogh. These were also the most heavily concentrated groups. While not proof of a charge into that area, it does increase the likelihood that they were attempting to clear the Horse Holder's Ravine area of infiltrating warriors.

Unfortunately for Captain Keogh and his battalion, three events began to rapidly unfold that would spell doom for them and eventually for Custer. The first thing to happen was the collapse of Company C's line. The warriors swept over Greasy Grass Ridge and rolled up the company's line. The two squads protecting Greasy Grass Ridge were clearly too few to hold off an attack by a large number of warriors or even as few as twenty for that matter. The short distance separating the opposing forces on that flank multiplied the advantage of numbers held by the warriors.

Most of the soldiers were unable to escape and died along Greasy Grass and Calhoun Ridges. The fight at Calhoun Ridge lasted only a very short time.[3] Sergeants Jeremiah Finley and George Finckle of Company C were killed while defending Calhoun Ridge. Their bodies were among many from that company found along Calhoun Ridge.

According to Little Hawk, a Northern Cheyenne warrior, the soldiers there were all dismounted to fight on foot. After an officer was killed and fell from his horse, the rest of the soldiers then mounted. Yellow Nose and Contrary Belly then made a charge, their second, which caused many of the soldiers to run. Yellow Nose later captured a company Guidon which he used to count coup on several soldiers.[4] The retreating soldiers first ran toward Company L (the nearest help) and then along Battle Ridge toward Custer Hill.[5]

The only company of the Keogh battalion that was led by only one officer was Company C. Lieutenant Henry M. Harrington's body was never identified which makes this account difficult to verify. Some believe that Lieutenant Harrington was a soldier that attempted to escape from the battlefield. The soldier was allegedly chased and killed by Crazy Horse. The soldiers closest to Company L ran to them for safety and probably continued over the hill and down to Keogh's new position in the low area where he was busy fending off the infiltrating warriors.

The men of Company L could not stem the tide of warriors charging in from the west as well as those to the south armed with lever action repeating rifles. They soon broke and ran towards Captain Keogh or across Battle

Ridge, in the direction of Custer Hill. The second and third events probably happened simultaneously or close to it. Either way, Keogh found himself in a low area engulfed by warriors on three sides.

The warriors chased the retreating soldiers, killing them as they would a herd of buffalo. Keogh was helpless to do anything but die in place with his most experienced men. Found near him were the bodies of his First Sergeant Frank E. Varden and First Sergeant Edwin Bobo of Company C who was probably reporting the collapse of his own company. The body of the remaining First Sergeant, James Butler of Company L, was found to the south of Calhoun Hill.[6]

Little Hawk's account is verified by Young Two Moon, another Northern Cheyenne warrior, who said that the company nearest the river (Company C) moved back toward the second company. The Sioux and Cheyenne then drove the three companies (C, L and I) across Battle Ridge towards the Gray Horse Company (Company E) on Custer Hill. Company E began to fire and drove the Indians off. This allowed a few men of Keogh's Battalion to reach Custer Hill.[7]

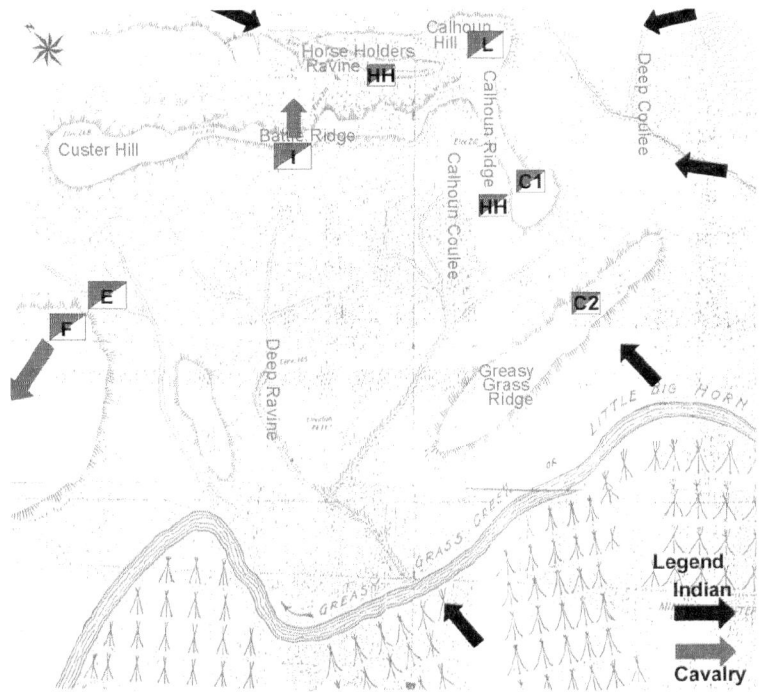

As Custer moves to the northwest with Companies F & E, the warriors begin to increase the pressure on Keogh's battalion.

Many of the soldiers are said to have thrown down their Springfield carbines. This should not be taken as a sign that their carbine ammunition was defective or depleted. Only one warrior mentioned finding a carbine with a round stuck in the breech. Many of the warriors later claimed that they found plenty of ammunition on the soldiers' bodies. The most likely explanation would be that the soldiers simply did not have time to reload when faced with numerous warriors at close quarters. The logical thing for them to do was utilize their revolvers for the short-range fighting.

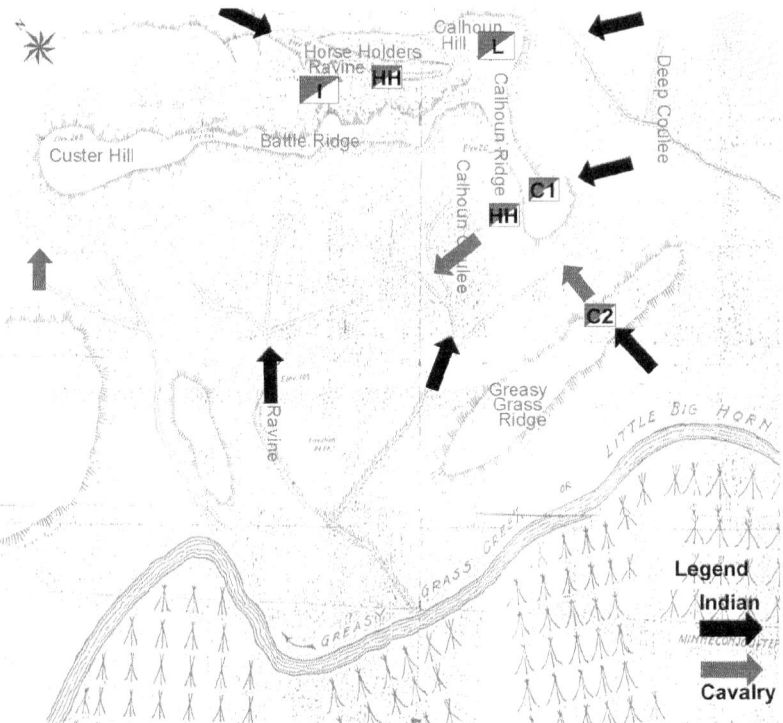

A group of about 80 warriors led by Crow King, attack the flank of soldiers on Greasy Grass Ridge. This attack causes a panic which forces the remnants of Company C to retreat toward Calhoun Hill.

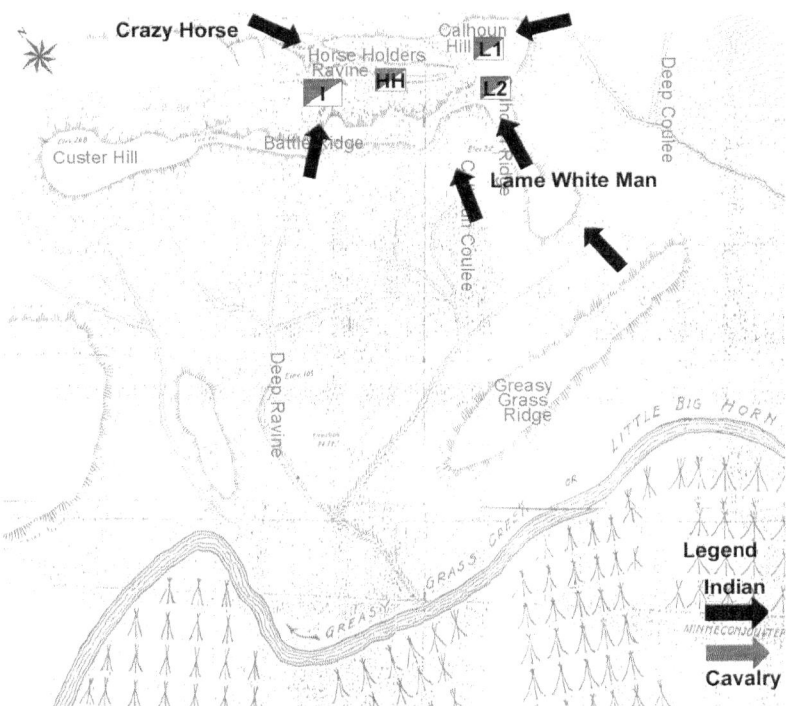

Without Company C to protect their right flank, the soldiers of Company L soon face attacks from several directions. They will soon begin to panic as well. Company I moves into the low area to the north of Calhoun Hill to protect Company L's horse holders. Company I will quickly be flanked as well.

The second event to occur may have involved Crazy Horse and his followers. It appears a large group of warriors rode up Deep Ravine from the river to Battle Ridge. These warriors cut off the retreating horse holders of Company C as they attempted to escape to the north. The movement through Deep Ravine to Battle Ridge placed these warriors directly behind both Calhoun and Keogh. Calhoun and his subaltern, Lieutenant John J. Crittenden (on loan from the Twentieth Infantry), would have fallen quickly as they were behind their company and closest to the warriors streaming up Deep Ravine.

The line in the Keogh sector had collapsed quickly as could be expected when soldiers suddenly find themselves facing a much larger force at close range and coming from multiple directions. The shock factor alone would have caused enough panic to make many of the soldiers run. At some point Crazy Horse made a bravery run in front of the soldiers. He rode in front of the soldier's line daring them to shoot him.

When it appeared that most of the soldiers had fired at Crazy Horse and missed, the other warriors took advantage of the soldiers' empty rifles. That charge separated the troops in the depression. This led to the final panic of Keogh's battalion. However, most of the men of Company I would not have had time to run. Those who did, found themselves running through a gauntlet of warriors in their futile attempt to reach safety. The collapse of Companies L and I probably happened within minutes of each other.

Lame White Man, a respected Cheyenne warrior, chased the men of Keogh's battalion from Calhoun Hill to Custer Hill. He and another warrior, Noisy Walking, were killed on the west side of Battle Ridge near Custer Hill. They were probably killed by soldiers from Company E who tried to protect the retreat of Keogh's men. Their bodies fell close to the soldiers. Lame White Man's body was mistaken for an Arikara scout by the Sioux warrior Little Crow, who took his scalp. He later returned it to Lame White Man's family with his apologies.[8]

The warriors were surprised when some of the soldiers attempted to give them their weapons and surrender. The warriors were not taking prisoners that day, which is not unusual considering they very rarely took adult male prisoners. They expected no mercy and gave none in return.[9]

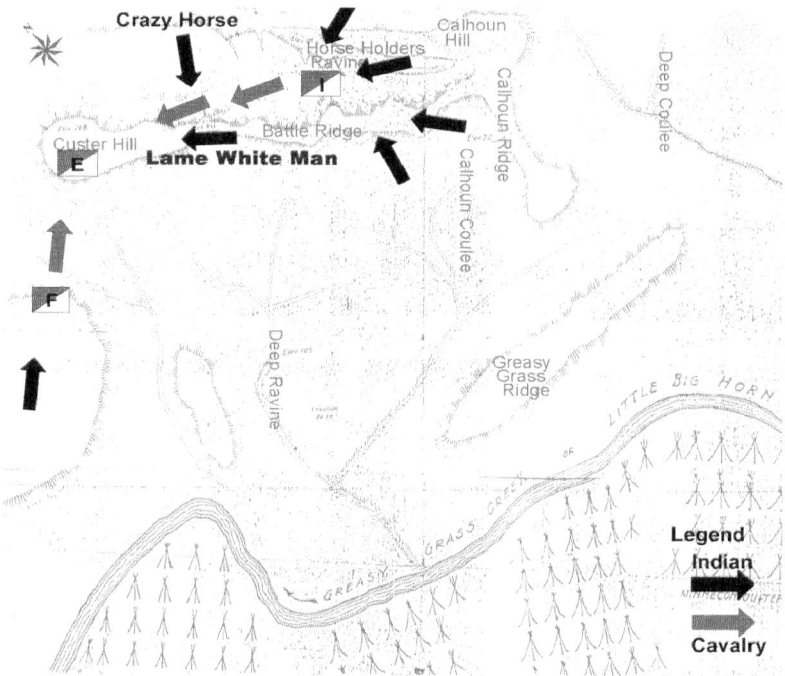

The soldiers of the Keogh battalion find themselves virtually surrounded in the low area. After Crazy Horse splits the remaining soldiers of the Keogh battalion they begin to run toward Company E, which was just returning to Custer Hill. Lame White Man gets too close to Company E and is killed.

Much of the fighting in the Keogh sector was reduced to close quarters combat. There was little opportunity for either side to do more than shoot at any movement. Some warriors were wounded by their own allies. The Keogh sector fighting lasted only a very short time. The companies were easily flanked and overwhelmed by superior numbers.

Panic set in quickly, and the warriors wisely took full advantage of the situation.

---

[1] Hardorff, The Custer Battle Casualties, II, pp. 127-129

[2] Hardorff, Lakota Recollections of the Custer Fight, pp. 147

[3] Ibid, pp. 146

[4] Hardorff, Lakota Recollections of the Custer Fight, pp. 140

[5] Jerome Greene, Lakota and Cheyenne, pp. 61-64

[6] Hardorff, The Custer Battle Casualties, pp. 108, 111, 117

[7] Ibid, pp. 68

[8] Hardorff, Cheyenne Memories of the Custer Fight, pp. 63, 90, 143

[9] Hyde, pp. 296

Panoramic photograph of the Keogh area taken by James Dulemba. The white specks are marble markers indicating the locations where the soldiers of Keogh's battalion were originally buried. The soldiers were evidently attempting to retreat from the low area on the right towards Custer Hill which is not in view to the left of the picture.

Lieutenant James Calhoun (left) and Lieutenant John J. Crittenden of the 20th Infantry, who was attached to Calhoun's Company L, would die with the men under their command on Calhoun Hill. Pictures courtesy of the LBHBNM.

Captain Myles Keogh, commanded a battalion at the Little Bighorn. This Irish born soldier of fortune would be killed with the men of his battalion. Courtesy of LBHBNM.

Another view of the Keogh area, this one from the southeast slope of Custer Hill. It shows more clearly the low area in which the remnants of the Keogh battalion became trapped. On the right is Battle Ridge. The ravine beginning at the right end of the ridge and moving toward the center of the picture is Horse Holder's Ravine, where Company L kept their horses. Picture courtesy of James Dulemba.

A view towards Custer Hill from the Keogh area. You can see the line of retreat by the marble markers of Captain Keogh's doomed soldiers. Courtesy of LBHBNM.

VIII. The Last Stand

When Custer left Keogh's battalion behind as a rear guard, he continued along Battle Ridge and then turned to the northwest from Custer Hill, angling toward the river. It is not known for certain what he saw in that direction to attack. Possibly, he caught sight of the retreating Indian non-combatants and hoped to capture some hostages. He was obviously unsuccessful because he would eventually return empty handed. He must have met with some resistance near the river which caused him to return to Custer Hill via the present day cemetery.

Newspaper reporter Mark Kellogg of the Bismarck Tribune and the New York Herald was killed on a side hill along the river northwest of the cemetery.[1] Owing to the fact that he was riding a mule, it is doubtful that he was killed attempting to escape from Custer Hill. The mule was reportedly slow, causing him to borrow Fred Gerard's spurs.[2] His body was not stripped but was scalped, making it likely that he was killed earlier than most of Yates' men, and his body was simply overlooked by the Indian women just as it nearly was by the burial party three days later. The significance of the position of his body is important because the cemetery is between that location and Custer Hill. It also shows that Yates' battalion advanced at least that far.

After an aborted attempt at crossing the river farther to the north, Company F was counter-attacked by warriors protecting the non-combatants. The warriors succeeded in scattering Company F's horses. Companies E and F were then forced to move back to Custer Hill in short movements. First one company would retreat while the other provided a covering fire to keep the enemy warriors from chasing them down from behind. Then they would switch roles so the second company could retreat.

Company E, commanded by Lieutenant Algernon E. Smith and his subaltern, Lieutenant James G. Sturgis, was extremely active during this segment of the battle. They were easily identified by the gray and white horses the company rode. The hostile warriors clearly remembered their movements for that reason. When Company E reached Custer Hill they dismounted and apparently gave covering fire for Captain George Yates' Company F.

Both of these companies probably witnessed the final destruction of Keogh's command, realizing then that their own fates were sealed as well. They did provide covering fire for the remnants of Keogh's battalion after Crazy Horse led the charge that split Keogh's line in two. However, they were only able to save a small portion of Keogh's command.

There was no safe area for horse holders to take the mounts so the soldiers attempted to hold their own. With the frightened horses jumping around, many of the soldiers' shots went straight up into the air or into the ground. Some of the warriors took advantage of the ridge lines to arc arrows into the soldiers' positions without exposing themselves to the erratic firing. Others simply moved in closer to kill the soldiers. As it was, the dust, gun smoke and confusion caused the warriors to kill or wound some of their own.

The officers would have made easy targets for the bullets and arrows of the warriors as some would probably have remained mounted or standing to direct the fire of their men. After most of the officers were killed or wounded, a large group of soldiers on foot and horseback began to retreat in the direction of the river. They were cut off from escape by warriors crawling up through the high grass and those who already occupied the area around the present cemetery.

Those soldiers that weren't killed changed course, fleeing south into Deep Ravine.[3] The warriors tell of one officer who attempted to cover the retreat of these soldiers. The officer fit the description of Captain Thomas Custer, but this individual could not be positively identified.[4] Soon after, a second, smaller group of soldiers attempted to follow the first group.

The warriors, observing this retreat from Custer Hill, decided the time was ripe to overrun the last defenders. They quickly killed those soldiers that showed any signs of life. The rest began to chase the men attempting to escape via Deep Ravine. Most were trapped in the ravine and killed like mice in a barrel. The "Last Stand" episode may have lasted less than twenty minutes. One or two chose to play dead for all the good that did, since they couldn't keep up the act for long once the women began to strip them of their clothes and mutilate their bodies.

One or two may have made it farther than the others due to the strength and speed of their horses. Corporal John Foley of Company C may have managed to make it into

Medicine Tail Coulee before being killed.[5] It is not known positively whether he was killed during the Medicine Tail Coulee episode or in the retreat from Custer Hill. His would be the body discovered closest to the ford by Benteen two days later. First Sergeant Butler of Company L may also have attempted his escape during this phase of the battle rather than during the collapse of the Keogh sector as mentioned earlier. Another viewpoint is that Butler was killed during the fighting in the Medicine Tail Coulee area earlier in the battle.

When all resistance on the Custer portion of the battlefield came to an end, the warriors began riding around shooting bullets and arrows into the bodies of the soldiers to ensure they were dead. Soldiers found wounded were generally beaten to death with stone clubs, axes or anything else that might be handy. Most of the bodies were stripped and mutilated to some extent.

Thanks to many past and present students of the battle, we have numerous accounts of the northern element of the battle. These accounts were given by the only people who witnessed the entire battle, the Indians. Unfortunately, because we do not share the same cultural views we do not always understand what they were trying to tell us.

The most valuable contribution the witnesses made was to give us a starting point, ending point, and the direction the battle flowed. Many of the Indian participants believed that both battalions fought as one group from Medicine Tail Coulee to Custer Hill, making several short stands along the way. Most of the participants did not see the separation of the battalions at Calhoun Hill. By the time they finished with Keogh's battalion, Custer had returned to Custer Hill. They probably just assumed that the Yates battalion had led the retreat.

The limited duration of the Custer fight should not be considered an indication of incompetence or cowardice on the part of the Custer battalions. Mistakes were certainly made and more than a few soldiers broke and ran. However, they were not prepared for the large numbers of warriors they were forced to face. Due to the broken terrain they attempted to defend, the separated companies were unable to provide effective supporting fire. This allowed the warriors to easily flank and rout each company in turn.

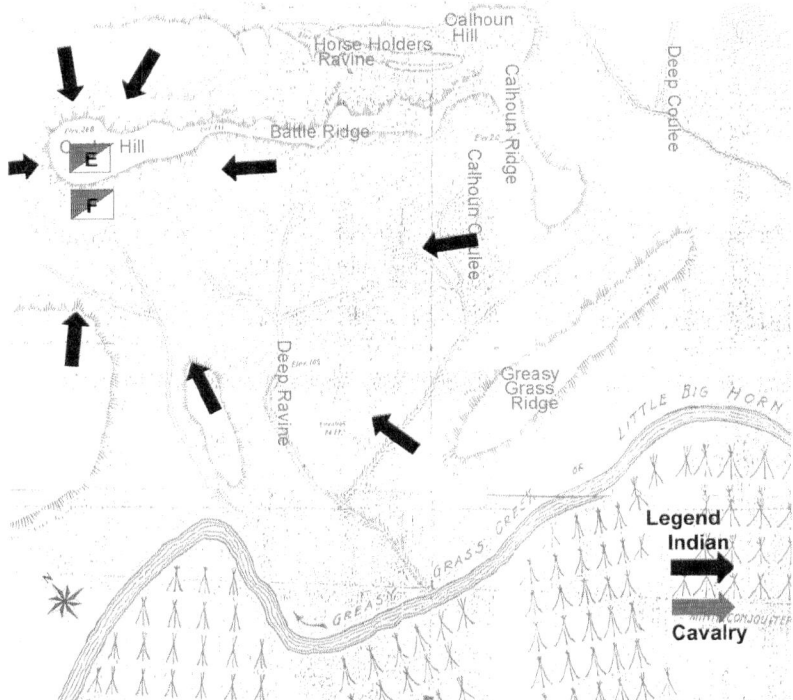

After returning to Custer Hill, the Yates battalion is quickly surrounded. The soldiers are unable to shoot accurately and control their horses as well. The warriors only needed to fire into the mass of men and soldiers in order to hit a target. Most of the officers will be killed or wounded leaving the remaining soldiers no hope of surviving on the hill.

The unorthodox style of warfare practiced by the Indians proved very effective against the largely inexperienced soldiers. While the soldiers usually stood up in the open, the warriors took advantage of the uneven terrain and high grass. Today we call it taking advantage of cover and concealment.

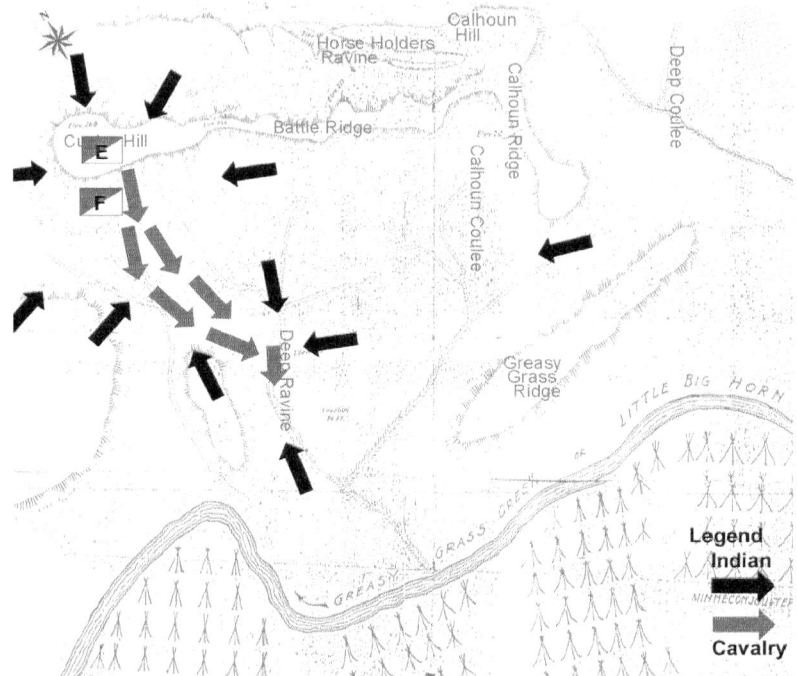

In desperation, the remaining soldiers attempt to reach the river. The warriors block the soldiers' path and force them to change direction. After being herded in Deep Ravine, the soldiers are quickly killed. Only Corporal Foley of Company C will escape the trap and make it to Medicine Tail Coulee before being killed. The wounded soldiers on Custer Hill are quickly overrun and killed.

The slow reloading time of the Springfield carbines carried by the soldiers, combined with the overwhelming number of warriors, also played a large role in the outcome of the Custer segment of the battle. We will never be sure how many warriors the Keogh and Yates battalions faced. However, it would seem that they fought at least one thousand five hundred warriors and possibly as many as three thousand.

The warriors had been capably led by Crazy Horse, Crow King, Gall, Iron Thunder, American Horse, Dull Knife, Lame White Man and Two Moon. Sitting Bull was a respected spiritual leader but not a war leader. His role in the battle was primarily to lend encouragement to his people. He was successful in stopping most of the early panic created by Major Reno's initial attack.

---

[1] Hardorff, The Custer Battle Casualties, pp. 121-122

[2] Hammer, pp. 231

[3] Ibid, pp. 207, 213

[4] Utley, Custer and the Great Controversy, pp. 112

[5] Hardorff, Lakota Recollections of the Custer Fight, pp. 114

Captain George Yates, commanded a battalion at the Little Bighorn. He was well liked by the other officers of the regiment, including Captain Benteen. Courtesy of LBHBNM.

Captain Thomas Ward Custer served as his brother's aide during the battle, giving command of his Company C to Lieutenant Harrington. Like his brother the General, Tom Custer was a courageous soldier, earning two Congressional Medals of Honor during the Civil War. Courtesy of LBHBNM.

The remains of these officers could not be identified after the battle.

Left: Lieutenant James Porter of Company I. Some of his bloody clothing was found in the village with bullet holes in them. Courtesy of James Dulemba.
Center: Lieutenant Henry Moore Harrington who commanded Company C during the battle. Courtesy of the Monroe County Historical Museum.
Right: Lieutenant James Sturgis was assigned to Company E during the battle. He was the son of Colonel Samuel Sturgis of the 7th Cavalry. Courtesy of James Dulemba.

Killed on Custer Hill with the General they were so loyal to. Pictures courtesy of James Dulemba.
Left: Lieutenant William Wyler Cooke, Adjutant of the 7th Cavalry.
Center: Lieutenant Algernon E. Smith commanded Company E during the battle.
Right: Lieutenant William Van Wyck Reily of Company F.

Custer Hill in 1877. In the foreground you can see a soldier's boot amongst the horse bones. Courtesy of LBHBNM.

George Custer (center) and the relatives who perished with him. Clockwise from upper left: Lieutenant James Calhoun (brother-in-law), Capt. Thomas Custer, Boston Custer and nephew Harry Reed. They would all perish within about half a mile of each other. Courtesy of LBHBNM.

Ogallala Sioux warrior Red Hawk fought at the Little Bighorn. Photograph taken by Edward S. Curtis in 1905. Courtesy Denver Public Library.

Left: Low Dog was reportedly the Ogallala Sioux warrior who stopped Corporal Foley from escaping the Custer fight. Courtesy of James Dulemba.
Center: Hunkpapa war leader Crow King led about 80 warriors in an attack against the rear of Company C's line on Calhoun Ridge. Courtesy of James Dulemba.
Right: Two Moon, one of the principle Cheyenne leaders. Courtesy of LBHBNM.

IX. Weir Point

When we left the Reno and Benteen battalions, they were waiting on the bluffs for the pack train to arrive. Almost immediately after the arrival of Benteen's battalions, some warriors began firing at the soldiers from nearby ravines, hills and bluffs. Their fire was ineffective, causing the soldiers no harm. Captain Weir's Company D was dismounted and used as skirmishers to drive them away. Lieutenant Godfrey's Company K was also dismounted and placed on the skirmish line. The Indians were soon observed departing of their own accord, riding down river.[1]

Once the firing ceased in the area around the bluffs, the officers and men of the two battalions began hearing the sounds of gunfire from down river. Major Reno seemed to be strangely obsessed with recovering Lieutenant Hodgson's body and personal effects, to the exclusion of all else.[2] This is a strong indicator that he was quite shaken from his defeat in the valley. He later seemed to recover his wits enough to take at least a minimal leadership role.

Captain Weir became anxious to move downstream and join Custer. After about ten minutes of pacing, he approached his subaltern, Lieutenant Edgerly, and asked him what he thought about taking Company D and riding to join Custer with or without the rest of the command.[3] Lieutenant Edgerly agreed, and Captain Weir went to request permission of Reno or Benteen. He and Reno allegedly argued over the answer, shouting at each other. Edgerly, however, claimed that Captain Weir later told him that he had not spoken to Reno or Benteen, but instead decided to ride out to the bluffs and look for Custer himself.[4]

Captain Weir returned to his company's area and retrieved his horse from his orderly. He mounted and rode off to the north without another word to anyone, his orderly following him. Lieutenant Edgerly, thinking that his commander had received permission to advance, mounted the rest of the company and followed. The company kept to the low areas while Captain Weir stayed along the higher ridge line. This movement began about thirty minutes after Benteen's battalion joined Reno's and just before the arrival of the pack train.[5] Both Lieutenant Hare and Captain McDougall both stated that Company D had already began to advance toward Custer but were still in sight when the pack train arrived.⁶

Traveling slowly, they would have arrived in the Weir Point area at approximately 5:10 p.m., which will become an important detail in determining the approximate ending time of the Custer fight. All that Weir, Edgerly and the men of Company D could see were vast numbers of Indians riding around shooting into unidentifiable objects on the ground. There was too much smoke and dust for them to see anything else from that distance as it was more than a mile just to Calhoun Hill.

Lieutenant Edgerly had apparently led Company D past Weir Point and north in the direction of Medicine Tail Coulee. When warriors began to move in the direction of Company D, Captain Weir signaled Lieutenant Edgerly to bring the company back. When Edgerly reached Weir Point, he observed Captain Benteen leading Companies M, K and his own H toward him. Lieutenant Hare, Reno's new adjutant, was observed conversing with Captain Weir. Apparently, Lieutenant Hare was giving an order to Captain Weir from Major Reno. It was to open up communications with Custer, if possible, and to inform the

General that Reno would join him as soon as the pack train had arrived.[7]

Captain McDougall guessed that the general movement of the combined command toward Custer began about one and one half hours after the pack train arrived. McDougall felt that Major Reno did not seem to grasp the seriousness of the situation.[8] It is quite probable that Captain McDougall overestimated the amount of time that had passed before the remaining six companies began to advance to the north. This is understandable for a couple of reasons. Nobody was looking at their watches so only very rough estimations of time were possible. When individuals estimate time they tend to err according to their level of patience and whether they are in a hurry or require more time. People forced to wait tend to overestimate the amount of time that has passed while those who require more time tend to underestimate the amount of time that has passed.

All of the soldiers who reached Weir Point agreed that the Indians from that direction came to attack them by the thousands. Even allowing for their exaggeration, it would seem that almost all of the warriors had to have moved to attack the joint Reno/Benteen battalions. Some would suggest that what Weir and his men saw on Calhoun Hill was only the collapse of L Company. The problem with that argument is that too many warriors were described as moving toward Weir Point to allow for the quick destruction of the remainder of Custer's men.

Lieutenant Godfrey testified in 1879 that, "When at Weir's Point I could see the general lay of the ground at the place of massacre, but could see no bodies or persons except Indians. I saw no evidence of fighting at that time."[9] All of the Indians interviewed described the movement back toward Reno as taking place after the destruction of Custer's two battalions.[10] The Sioux warrior, Gall, verified that Custer's men were all dead by the time Weir's Company reached the high ground at Weir Point.[11] Gall's statement is verified by other warriors interviewed during the years after the battle.

There was never any mention by any of the troops that reached Weir Point of seeing any soldiers retreating into Medicine Tail Coulee. This would seem to verify that Gall spoke truthfully and both Corporal Foley and First Sergeant Butler were already dead. It would also suggest that the Custer fight was over by at least five minutes before

Company D reached the Weir Point area. Another reason for believing Gall is that none of the soldiers ever mentioned hearing any more shooting from that direction after the Indians began to pursue Company D.[12]

If we figure that the Custer fight began in Medicine Tail Coulee a few minutes after Reno's retreat from the wooded area, we have an estimated time of 3:55 p.m. If we place the end time at approximately 5:05 p.m., we can estimate that Custer's battle only lasted about an hour and ten minutes after Reno reached the bluffs. If we believe Trumpeter Martin's statement, Custer's fight began around 3:25 p.m. and lasted about one hour and forty minutes. Either way, the fight was of short duration.

Lieutenant DeRudio, Private Thomas O'Neill, Fred Gerard and William Jackson hid in the timber during Reno's retreat. All four would eventually return to Reno's command. Lieutenant DeRudio and Private O'Neill both spoke of hearing the firing from Custer's fight. Private O'Neill told interviewer Walter Camp that the firing from Custer's direction ended at about 5:00 p.m.[13]

Major Reno was attempting to organize the remnants of the remaining companies and the pack train. The wounded were still on the bluffs as Captain Moylan was having trouble moving them. Captain McDougall let Moylan have one of his two platoons to help with transporting the wounded.[14] Some of the soldiers were without mounts, and George Herendeen arrived with about a dozen soldiers who had followed him back across the river on foot after the bulk of the warriors had moved down river. These men had wisely hidden until then. A few more soldiers, Privates Peter Thompson and James Watson of Company C, also made surprise appearances.

Twenty-six excess men from the doomed companies ended up with Reno and Benteen on the hilltop. It is unlikely that all of their horses gave out, but the army only questioned the survival of Private Gustav Korn after the battle. A few may have had reasonable excuses but not all of them. We will never know how many extra men from the Reno and Benteen battalions were with the pack train because they ended up with their companies in the end.

After about an hour at Weir Point, with the large numbers of warriors moving toward the soldiers, the order to fall back to the bluffs was given. The order probably originated with Captain Benteen, who also ordered

Company M to cover Weir's retreat, but they did not wait long before they retreated themselves.[15] During the retreat, Farrier Vincent Charley of Company D was shot through both hips and fell from his horse. He attempted to crawl along with the rest of his company begging his friends not to leave him.

Lieutenant Edgerly and Sergeant Thomas Harrison stopped momentarily, and the Lieutenant told Charley to hide in a ravine until he could return with some men to save him. By this time, the first warriors were within fifty yards of them and closing fast. Lieutenant Edgerly and Sergeant Harrison retreated only to hear the warriors finish off Charley moments later.[16] They would find Vincent Charley's body two days later. He was the only soldier killed during the retreat from Weir Point.

Lieutenant Godfrey formed Company K into a skirmish line about two hundred yards from the defensive position which was already being formed on the bluffs. Godfrey sent his company's horses to the rear and held back the warriors long enough to give the other companies a chance to organize. Finally, Godfrey was ordered to retreat and fill in the defensive perimeter's northeastern line between Companies D and M.

Major Reno and Captain Benteen instructed the company commanders where to place their men and for the most part left them to run their commands. This defensive position was located in the same area that Major Reno retreated to after withdrawing from the valley. The horses and pack mules were placed in a small depression near the middle of the line. The wounded were also placed there for protection and were under the care of the sole surviving surgeon, Dr. Henry R. Porter. The next engagement began almost immediately as the warriors surrounded their defensive position. This would be the third round of fighting for the day.

---

[1] Graham, The Reno Court Of Inquiry, pp. 160, 177

[2] Godfrey, pp. 26

[3] Graham, The Reno Court of Inquiry, pp. 160-161

[4] George M. Clark, Scalp Dance, pp. 19

[5] Ibid, pp. 161

[6] Hammer, pp. 66, 70

[7] Graham, The Reno Court Of Inquiry, pp. 95 ; Hammer, pp. 56

[8] Hammer, pp. 70

[9] Graham, The Reno Court Of Inquiry, pp. 186

[10] Ibid, pp. 207, 210

[11] Edgar I. Stewart, Custer's Luck, pp. 397

[12] Graham, The Reno Court Of Inquiry, pp. 173, 180

[13] Hammer, pp. 108

[14] Graham, The Reno Court Of Inquiry, pp. 194

[15] Carroll, pp. 216

[16] Camp, pp. 97-99

Captain Benteen's Officers

Clockwise from upper left: Captain Thomas Weir (commanded Company D), Lieutenant Winfield Scott Edgerly (Company D), Lieutenant Edward Godfrey (commanded Company K) and Lieutenant Francis M. Gibson (Company H). Pictures Courtesy of LBHBNM.

Sioux warrior Gall indicated Custer's men were dead before the Weir Point episode. Courtesy of Little Bighorn Battlefield National Monument.

X. The Hilltop Fight

While the soldiers were still trying to get organized, one of the pack mules carrying two thousand rounds of ammunition broke loose and ran toward the Indians. The mule was gallantly retrieved by Sergeant Richard Hanley of Company C who mounted his horse and herded the frightened mule back toward his comrades. The sergeant came under heavy fire from the warriors during this action.[1] He would later be awarded the Congressional Medal of Honor for his valorous act.

Major Reno and Captain Benteen walked the line to make sure the troops were placed as advantageously as possible. Captain McDougall's Company B faced the bluffs to the west with Company H on the far southern flank and Captain French's Company M faced the north. Company K was also placed on the northern flank with Company D on their right flank facing east. The remnants of Company G, now commanded by Lieutenant Wallace and Company A also faced the warriors to the east. Additionally, there were sixty-one men from Custer's five companies positioned on the hilltop.

The situation was desperate. If even one section of the line broke, the whole position would soon follow. Many of the men assumed that it was only a matter of time before they were all killed. On several occasions, Benteen and Reno had to run the packers and the skulkers out of the pack train area and back to the perimeter.

There was little cover to be found, and almost every position was exposed to fire from several directions. The warriors kept up heavy fire on the soldiers until it was too dark to see. Before the firing stopped for the night at about 9:00 p.m., seven more soldiers were killed and twenty-one wounded.[2] Many of the soldiers used the night's respite to dig firing pits in the poor soil. This chore was made more difficult by the fact that there were only a few shovels in the entire command. The men used their knives and any other utensils available to dig with.

Benteen's Company H failed to dig in and paid dearly for it the next day. They would suffer the most casualties during the hilltop defense. Captain Benteen received a great deal of criticism for not making his men dig in during the night of the 25th. It was a mistake he later acknowledged.

Major Reno would again be forced to run some of the civilian packers back out to the perimeter. Though the packers were not paid to fight, every able bodied man was expected to help defend the perimeter. Even some of the wounded returned to the line on their own accord. Some felt that the hospital area was no safer than being on the perimeter.

During the night, the defenders heard the sounds of at least one army trumpet. Major Reno ordered Trumpeter Martin to sound recall and some other trumpet calls believing he was alerting Custer or whoever else it might be of their whereabouts. They received no recognizable military response and finally gave up.[3] The trumpet they heard had been taken from Custer's dead and was no doubt played by a warrior or an Indian boy.

The soldiers could see large fires burning in the village. They could also hear what sounded like happy singing that they attributed to a big celebration in the village. In actuality, the village was mourning its own losses.[4] The Indians had lost very few warriors in comparison to the soldiers but had also lost some women and children. Both of Gall's wives had been killed as well as his three children.

While some would call this an example of the Army's policy of exterminating all Indians, it was actually an example of poor marksmanship on the part of the soldiers. Reno's men had typically fired too high when shooting at the warriors and unfortunately struck women, children, tepees and anything else that would stop a bullet. Lodges caught fire when stray bullets hit lodge poles causing some to collapse onto the cooking fires inside. These burning lodges caused some to believe that Major Reno's battalion had actually made it into the village only to be forced back out.

Many of the officers and men on the hilltop believed that Custer had retreated to the north in hopes of joining forces with General Terry who was traveling with Colonel John Gibbon's column. Colonel Gibbon's column was comprised of four companies of the 2nd Cavalry and six companies of the 7th Infantry. Additionally, a small detachment of men from the 20th Infantry and three Gatling guns also traveled with Colonel Gibbon's column. This detachment was commanded by a Lieutenant Low.

Gibbon's Montana Column was traveling south along the Bighorn River in the hopes of blocking the Indians' escape to the north.

Some of the officers and men felt that they had been deserted by Custer and left to their fates. Others felt that Custer was probably pinned down as they were with wounded that couldn't be left behind. Major Reno knew of General Terry's plan to wait at the junction of the Bighorn and Little Bighorn Rivers. The officers on the hilltop felt that Custer could take care of himself as well as they could.[5]

Lieutenant Varnum volunteered to attempt to take a message to Custer. Major Reno declined the offer believing that only another Indian could slip through the cordon of Sioux and Cheyenne warriors. He asked the Crow scouts to try to escape with a message. Two of them were given messages after agreeing, but they didn't get very far before turning back. They believed there were too many Sioux watching for anyone to escape.[6]

After entrenching and putting up barricades of boxes, packsaddles, sides of bacon, dead horses and mules, picket guards were placed about three hundred yards in front of

Company A's lines. Six Privates and one Corporal, Stanislas Roy, kept watch in two hour shifts. The Privates would sit rather than stand in order to remain less visible and avoid drawing enemy fire.[7] Although not mentioned, it is likely that some of the other companies placed picket guards out as well.

---

[1] Nichols, Men With Custer, pp. 138

[2] Nichols, In Custer's Shadow, pp. 196

[3] Camp, pp. 92

[4] Marquis, Wooden Leg, pp. 255-257

[5] Graham, The Reno Court of Inquiry, pp. 219

[6] Godfrey, pp. 30

[7] Taylor, pp. 52-54

Left: Lieutenant George E. Lord, Assistant Surgeon. Dr. Lord was killed with the soldiers of the Yates battalion. Courtesy of LBHBNM.
Center: Dr. Henry Porter was the only surgeon to survive the battle. His excellent care saved the lives of many of the soldiers on the bluffs. Courtesy of James Dulemba.
Right: Dr. James DeWolf was assigned to the Reno battalion. He was killed during the retreat to the bluffs. Courtesy of LBHBNM.

XI. Day Two

Major Reno ordered Trumpeter Martin to sound reveille at 2:00 a.m. Within the hour, two shots were fired signaling the beginning of the day's siege. The two shots were followed by heavy firing from the warriors who, once again, occupied just about every ridge and coulee within six hundred yards of Major Reno's defensive perimeter. The picket guards quickly returned to their company lines. Many of the warriors used the cover of darkness to climb up the bluffs on foot. They were able to crawl close enough to some of the soldiers to throw rocks and small arrows at them.[1]

The warriors kept up their heavy fire for several hours. The pauses were generally filled with attempts to charge the perimeter. It wasn't until about 10:00 a.m. that the shooting slackened considerably. The Indian warriors probably began to get bored with the siege of the remaining soldiers. Sharpshooter's Ridge, to the north, had a clear view of most of the soldier positions. Warriors located along that ridge probably caused most of the hilltop casualties. They could easily shoot into the flanks of the troops facing the bluffs and into the backs of Benteen's men. The soldiers did their best to keep their heads down until the warriors attempted a charge.

Benteen's company began suffering a high casualty rate causing the captain to once again look for skulkers hiding with the pack mules. He had his men take packs and saddles back to their lines to fortify their positions.[2] Soldiers from Company A helped carry some of the packs and saddles over to Company H's lines.

Because of the warrior positions on the higher ground on Sharpshooter's Ridge, nobody was safe, whether hiding in a shallow trench, behind a pack saddle, or behind hardtack boxes. Several of the soldiers killed on the hilltop were killed while lying down behind cover or in a shallow trench. Private Henry C. Voight of Company M was shot through the head and killed while trying to untangle a wounded horse from the others.[3] Civilian Packer Frank C. Mann was killed while shooting from a position along Company A's lines.[4] In contrast, Captain Benteen reportedly spent most of the 26th standing up and walking the perimeter.[5] He only received a scratch on his thumb and had one boot heel shot off.

After Company H's casualties began to increase Benteen finally went to Major Reno and requested that another company be assigned to support his own. Captain French's Company M was assigned to reinforce them. Soon after, Captain Benteen led both companies in a charge against the Indians in a ravine leading down the bluffs to the river.[6] The warriors had been too close to Benteen's area of the perimeter, and he realized that if they were allowed to stay there long enough they might eventually overrun his line. The warriors reportedly ran down the steep ravine, almost turning somersaults in their efforts to escape the soldiers' charge.

One of the few casualties of the charge was Private James Tanner of Company M. He was mortally wounded while returning to the perimeter after the charge. A Sioux warrior named Long Road showed great courage in counting coups on Tanner, who was lying fairly close to his comrades. Indians believed that it took greater courage to touch an enemy than it did to kill an enemy. They referred to this act as counting coup. The first and second warriors to touch a dead or wounded enemy would be credited with the coup. Long Road was killed during this act of bravery, and his body was far too close to the soldiers to be recovered by his friends. First Sergeant John Ryan of Company M and three other men ran out to rescue Private Tanner by lifting him onto a blanket and carrying him back to the field hospital.[7] Private Tanner died a short time later from his wound.

With the warriors pushed back from his own side of the perimeter, Captain Benteen observed that the warriors were beginning to establish themselves around Major Reno's side of the perimeter. He informed Reno of the situation and advised him to charge and clear them out as he had done. Reno led the charge, and the warriors were sent running.[8] These charges served more than one purpose, as we shall soon see.

As the firing eased for awhile, the cries of the wounded for water became the next concern for the soldiers. Heat, dust, gunpowder, loss of blood, and fear all increase an individual's thirst. The other soldiers were thirsty as well, so it was clear to everyone that something had to be done soon to secure water for the men. Soldiers were requested to volunteer and about two dozen came forward at various times of the day. Some made more than one trip to the river for the precious liquid. The ravine cleared by Benteen's charge was used by the water carriers to reach the river.[9]

The volunteers gathered camp kettles, cooking pots, canteens and anything else that would hold water. Their path down Water Carrier's Ravine was the easy part of their dangerous mission. The bends in the trail provided cover and concealment from the warriors on the other side of the river. The real danger came in the final thirty feet to the river which was open ground. The volunteers were completely exposed to enemy fire for that thirty foot run. They were also exposed during the time required to lie down next to the river filling their water vessels.

After filling their containers they had to run back to the safety of the bend in the ravine. Due to the poor marksmanship of the warriors, most of the volunteers made it safely. Some were not so fortunate. A few were killed and some were wounded.[10]

Saddler Michael Madden of Company K was shot below the knee in his attempt to get water. He had to be carried back up the ravine to the hospital area. Dr. Porter was forced to amputate Madden's leg. After receiving some brandy before and after the surgery, the heavy drinking

Madden jokingly told the doctor to cut off his good leg. Many soldiers had nothing better to do with their free time so they would get drunk. Michael Madden was just such a soldier. Madden would receive a promotion to sergeant and a position as a harness maker at the department headquarters in St. Paul, Minnesota after his medical discharge from the Army.[11]

Private Peter Thompson of Company C reportedly made six trips for water. The trips were all made after receiving a wound to his right hand. He would receive the Congressional Medal of Honor for his heroism on behalf of his fellow soldiers.[12] Private Thompson as you may recall was one of the Company C soldiers whose horse gave out between the North Fork of Reno Creek and Reno Hill. Gustave Korn reportedly brought more water to the wounded than anyone else.[13] Unlike most of his fellow water carriers, he was not awarded the Medal of Honor for his actions. Few of the soldiers from the companies whose commanding officers were killed, were awarded the medal. Officers probably felt little obligation to seek awards for the soldiers from other companies.

After some of the water carriers had been wounded, Captain Benteen found four volunteers to act as sharpshooters to provide cover fire for future trips to the river. Sergeant George Geiger, Henry Mechling, Otto Voit and Private Charles Windolph, all from Company H, drew fire away from the water carriers. They stood up along the bluffs overlooking the river and fired at the warriors hiding in the trees on the opposite bank. They, too, would receive Medals of Honor for their gallantry. Private Windolph would also receive a promotion to sergeant from Captain Benteen. He remained loyal to Benteen until the day he died.[14]

Although the heavy firing of the warriors became lighter around 10:00 a.m., it would occasionally become heavier. Many of the warriors had apparently expended a great deal of their ammunition. Modern rancher Henry Weibert, who lived most of his life in the area, found numerous cartridge casings in the battlefield area. He also found several in positions that belonged to the warriors surrounding the soldiers' hilltop position. They indicated that they had been fired from the wrong caliber rifles. This might indicate that some had run out of ammunition for their rifles and had to borrow shells from other warriors.[15]

There are other reasons for the slackening in the warriors' firing. Some of the warriors may have grown bored with the hilltop fight, and the village may also have received word of General Terry's movement up the Bighorn River. Later in the day, they would confront him about six miles away from the scene of Custer's defeat. Some of these warriors would return to the Reno area from time to time and the fight would heat up again for a few minutes. By late afternoon, few warriors remained to watch the soldiers while the village moved south. The grass in the valley was set on fire to keep the soldiers from following and possibly, to burn out any white survivors still hiding in the grove of trees along the west side of the river.[16]

By the time General Terry had reached his agreed upon position near the junction of the Bighorn and Little Bighorn Rivers, a large number of warriors were there to confront his force of less than four hundred men. Rather than risk an ambush, General Terry set up a defensive line and set up a camp after the warriors chose not to attack.[17] This camp was only about three miles from Custer Hill. The warriors backed away and joined the rest of the village in its migration south.

Major Reno's officers and men were able to view much of the village's departure from the valley. The site left them in awe as they saw their opponents' numbers for the first time. Captain Benteen estimated that there were 1,800 warriors and a pony herd consisting of about 20,000.[18] In his official report, General Terry stated that Reno and Benteen had estimated the number of warriors "at not less than twenty-five hundred."[19] The village was estimated to be about three miles long and half a mile wide in some places. It was probably much smaller as exaggeration under such circumstances is quite normal.

After the village's departure, Major Reno ordered the perimeter moved farther south in order to get away from the smell of dead men and animals. The dead were buried in the shallow rifle pits of the old positions. Lieutenant Hodgson's body was recovered and buried as well. The horses and mules were culled to separate those that would survive from those that would have to be destroyed. The surviving animals were taken down to the river in groups. It was the first water they had received in more than 24 hours.[20] Guards were posted as the officers were not sure whether or not the departure of the village was just a trick to draw the soldiers from their defensive positions.

During the early morning hours of June 27th, four more survivors of the valley fight hailed the troops on the hilltop. Interpreter Fred Gerard and scout William Jackson returned after midnight. Lieutenant Charles DeRudio and Private Thomas O'Neill returned at about 2:00 a.m. The four had initially hidden together until they had run into a party of hostile warriors on the evening of June 25th.

After separating from the two civilians, Lieutenant DeRudio and Private O'Neill hid out in the trees along the river. They moved farther to the south until they reached the area where Major Reno's battalion had crossed the river to attack the village. After dark on the night of the 26th, they crossed the river with the intention of walking back to the supply depot on the Powder River. They turned toward Reno's hilltop position only after they heard the sound of a mule.[21]

With the battle over, there was time to take a tally of the dead, wounded and missing. Thirteen officers and 334 enlisted men had defended the hilltop position. Seventeen men had been killed in the hilltop fight and forty-three more had been wounded, including Lieutenant Varnum. The lieutenant had been slightly wounded in both legs.

Three more men would die from their wounds on the return trip to Fort Abraham Lincoln. Two others succumbed to their wounds at the fort. Three officers and twenty-nine enlisted men were killed and seven were wounded in the valley fight. Three civilians: Charley Reynolds, Isaiah Dorman and F. C. Mann, as well as three Arikara scouts were killed in the valley and hilltop fights.[22] The total loss for the Seventh Cavalry was yet to be known by the survivors of the hilltop fight.

---

[1] Graham, The Reno Court of Inquiry, pp. 141-142

[2] Ibid, pp. 141

[3] Hammer, pp. 136

[4] Taylor, pp. 58

[5] Charles Windolph, I Fought With Custer, pp. 103-105

[6] Ibid, pp. 105-106

[7] Sandy Barnard, Custer's First Sergeant John Ryan, pp. 190-191; Nichols, In Custer's Shadow, pp. 201

[8] Nichols, In Custer's Shadow, pp. 201

[9] Camp, pp. 109-112

[10] Graham, The Custer Myth, pp. 145

[11] E.A. Brininstool, Troopers With Custer, pp. 57-59, 228-230

[12] Nichols, Men With Custer, pp.329

[13] Ibid, pp. 183-184

[14] Windolph, pp. 104-105

[15] Henry and Don Weibert, Sixty-six Years in Custer's Shadow, pp. 111

[16] Cyrus Townsend Brady, Indian Fights and Fighters, pp. 252

[17] James H. Bradley, The March of the Montana Column, pp. 157-160

[18] Gray, Centennial Campaign, pp. 355

[19] Dustin, pp. 180

[20] Stewart, pp. 429

[21] Hammer, pp. 108-110, pp. 233-236

[22] Nichols, <u>Men With Custer</u>, pp. 374-391

XII. Aftermath

On Tuesday morning, June 27, 1876, the remnants of the Seventh Cavalry enjoyed their first regular breakfast since June 24th. They were able to properly care for their horses and pack mules as well. Major Reno continued to hold his command in readiness should the hostile warriors return. There were none in sight, but they could see some horses grazing in the valley below, and there was no certainty that they were out of danger.

At about 9:30 a.m., dust was observed in the distance down river (north). Assembly was sounded by Trumpeter Martin. The water containers were quickly filled, and the animals were once again placed in a protected area. After some suspense during the wait to determine who was approaching, the defenders recognized the slow advance of a column of soldiers. The question then became whose column was approaching? Was it Custer returning with his five companies? Was it General Terry with Colonel Gibbon's column? Was it General George Crook's Wyoming column?

Muggins Taylor, a scout for Colonel Gibbon's column, arrived first with a message for General Custer from General Terry. The note informed them that some of Custer's Crow Scouts had found General Terry. They had informed General Terry that Custer had been defeated, and only a few survivors were left. Terry indicated his disbelief but informed them that he was coming with medical help just in case. Major Reno sent Lieutenants Varnum and Hare with some of the enlisted men to guide General Terry to the bluffs.[1]

At about 10:30 a.m., General Terry, Colonel Gibbon and Gibbon's Chief of Scouts, Lieutenant James Bradley, arrived at Reno's camp. The officers and enlisted men of the Seventh Cavalry were anxious to know of General Custer's whereabouts. They asked General Terry if he had any word from Custer or knew of his location. Terry had the solemn task of informing them that Lieutenant Bradley had found Custer and all those with him dead. The bodies of General Custer and his five companies were located four miles to the north.[2]

The stunned command couldn't believe the news. Captain Benteen expressed his disbelief out loud and was invited by General Terry to take a look for himself. Major Reno gave him permission to take H Company and some of the other officers with him. Lieutenant Bradley guided Captain Benteen, Captain Weir, Lieutenant Godfrey and Company H to Custer's field. Upon reaching a high ridge, most likely around Weir Point, they could see a large number of white boulders in the distance. After utilizing field glasses, they realized that the boulders were actually the naked bodies of Custer's men. Captain Weir exclaimed in horror, "Oh, how white they look! How white!"[3]

The first body found was located about six hundred yards from Medicine Tail Ford which they believed Custer had attempted to use to cross the river. All but a few of the bodies were stripped of clothing. Most of them were scalped or otherwise mutilated. The term "mutilation" can be misleading as many of the crushed skulls of the dead were the result of blows from war clubs to finish off the wounded rather than to purposely disfigure the dead. It is possible that many of those found in such condition were still alive when the hostile warriors reached them. Some may have been unconscious while others saw what was coming, but were too injured to resist. War clubs would also have been used on those attempting to surrender. It may sound callous, but for a warrior, bullets were expensive and hard to obtain.

The condition of General George Custer's corpse differs depending upon which survivor you believe. Most agreed that he was stripped of his clothing. Charles Windolph always maintained that he was found fully clothed. Some would have us believe he appeared to be only asleep. Most claimed that he was not mutilated while a few later admitted that he had some minor mutilations to his corpse. Descriptions of the particular mutilations are unnecessary as they can't be confirmed at this late date, nor are they relevant to the outcome of the battle. His body was found very close to the southern edge of the present monument.

Captain Thomas Custer's body was found nearby. He had been so badly disfigured that identification could only be made by his initials tattooed on his wrist. Judging from the degree of mutilation, Captain Custer was most likely alive and resisting when the warriors overran Custer Hill.[4] Some of the tales told by the Sioux and Cheyenne warriors support that theory.

The only company officers that could definitely be said to have died with their companies were Captain Keogh, Captain Yates, Lieutenants Calhoun, Crittenden and William Van Wyck Reily. The others were either not identified or their commands were scattered over too large of an area to be sure. It is very likely that Company E retreated toward Deep Ravine after the deaths of all or most of the officers on Custer Hill. The others that followed would also have realized the hopelessness of defending the hill.

We believe we understand how the men of the Keogh and Yates battalions ended up scattered all over the field with little resemblance of company defensive formations. Captain Benteen and the other survivors could not recognize many signs of organized resistance. Benteen was convinced that General Custer's fight had been nothing more than a panicked rout with many orders given but few obeyed.[5] It is likely that the other officers believed the same. While they were not completely correct, they were not entirely wrong, either. This misinterpretation would have a profound effect on how the survivors answered questions regarding the battle.

Captain Benteen and the others made a quick count of the bodies and attempted to identify the dead officers. The bodies of Lieutenants James Porter of Company I, Harrington of C, James Sturgis of E and Dr. George E. Lord were not identified. Dr. Lord's identification is open to debate. Some claimed they had identified his body while others claimed differently. It is just another one of the many inconsistencies involving this battle.

The rest of the survivors waited in suspense for Benteen's return. They wanted to know about their friends and their commander. Benteen told them of his observations and his count. With the number of unaccounted for bodies, there was some hope that a few individuals had escaped. No legitimate survivors of the Custer fight ever came forward with the exception of the young Crow scout, Curly, who made his escape during the early stages of the Custer fight. The hilltop survivors would get to see more than they ever wanted of Custer's field on the following day. Most of them would never be able to get the gruesome visions of that battlefield out of their heads.

The remainder of June 27th was spent moving the wounded across the river to General Terry's camp and destroying all extra or damaged equipment. Any government property that could not be carried and might prove of some use to the Indians was placed in one location on the hill and destroyed. Nothing was to be left for the Indians to find and use.

The bodies of those killed in the valley fight were buried by Colonel Gibbon's troops. Lieutenant McIntosh's body was identified by his brother-in-law, Lieutenant Francis Gibson of Company H.[6] They were married to sisters. Gibbon's troops would camp in the vicinity of the valley fight and had to bury the bodies or tolerate the stench of decaying humans and horses. Reno's valley dead were even more badly mutilated than Custer's. They fell close to the village, and the Indians were well aware that it was the soldiers of this group that were responsible for the deaths of the few women and children killed during the battle.

The Seventh Cavalry spent most of June 28th burying their dead on Custer's field. The job was too gruesome to fully describe. There were few shovels to go around. The bodies were badly decomposed after almost three full days lying out in the hot sun. Attempts at moving the bodies found in Deep Ravine were futile due to the condition of the bodies. The ground was hard and flaked when attempts were made to dig. This made covering the bodies harder still.

Many of the dead had little more than a shovel of dirt thrown over them. George and Tom Custer probably received the best burials. They were placed in an eighteen inch deep trench and were wrapped in canvas and blankets. They were then covered with the dirt from the hole. The basket portion of an Indian travois was placed upside down over the grave, and the sides were held down with stones around the edges to keep the wild animals from digging them up.[7]

The men in Deep Ravine had the sides of the ravine collapsed over their bodies. The officers' bodies were marked for future reburial. The enlisted men's graves were not marked with the possible exception of some of the non-commissioned officers such as Sergeant Major Sharrow and the company first sergeants. Even the identification of Sergeant Major Sharrow's body is uncertain at best. This was typical of the military during that era.

The burial parties could not work long without becoming ill. They would often stumble down to the river to be sick and drink water. The sites were bad enough on their own, but the smells made the job even more unbearable.[8] They would work in shifts lasting approximately thirty minutes. There was not time enough to do a more thorough job. The wounded needed to be moved fifteen miles, to the Far West, one of the two river boats that had been hired to carry supplies for the expedition.

The Far West, commanded by Captain Grant Marsh, was waiting at the junction of the Bighorn and Little Bighorn Rivers. The combined columns would spend the 29th making litters for transporting the wounded. Blanket stretchers were initially used to carry the wounded but proved inadequate for the job. Stretchers were eventually hung between pairs of mules which proved more satisfactory for the difficult task.[9]

The Far West arrived at the wharf at Bismarck, Dakota Territory, at 11:00 p.m. on July 5th, 1876. It was a trip of nearly one thousand miles completed in just fifty-four hours. Fort Lincoln, the 7th Cavalry's home, was across the

Missouri River from Bismarck. The steam boat made it back to Fort Abraham Lincoln, Dakota Territory, in record time, but three of the wounded died en route: Corporal George H. King, Private James C. Bennett and Private William M. George. Two more, Privates David Cooney and Frank Braun would succumb to their wounds at the fort.[10]

A breakdown of those who died of their wounds is listed on the following pages by unit in Tables 1 and 2. The Headquarters staff does not count Captain Thomas Custer or the two Colors Sergeants, who are listed with their assigned companies. All of the officers killed in action are listed with the companies to which they were actually assigned with the exception of Lieutenant Crittenden of the Twentieth Infantry who was attached to Company L.

Table 1: Soldiers

Unit	Killed	Wounded	Died of Wounds
HQ	6	0	0
Co. A	9	7	1
Co. B	3	5	1
Co. C	39	4	1
Co. D	3	3	0
Co. E	38	2	0
Co. F	37	0	0
Co. G	14	6	0
Co. H	3	20	1
Co. I	38	1	1
Co. K	5	3	0
Co. L	45	1	0
Co. M	13	11	1
Total	253	63	6

Table 2: Attachments

Unit	Killed	Wounded	Died of Wounds
Scouts	2	2	0
Guides	3	0	0
Interpreters	2	0	0
Correspondents	1	0	0
Citizens	1	0	0
Packers	1	1	0
Total	10	3	0

The total dead for the Seventh Cavalry and their attachments numbered 269. The wounded that survived totaled 66.[11] It was a terrible defeat for the United States Army but it would also mark the beginning of the end for the Plains Indian tribes. The battle was over, but the campaign would go on for another year. Ironically, in defeat, the Seventh Cavalry rode into glory while the victorious Sioux, Cheyenne and Arapaho tribes were eventually hunted down and forced onto reservations.

---

[1] Godfrey, pp. 35-36

[2] Nichols, In Custer's Shadow, pp. 205

[3] Godfrey, pp. 38

[4] Hammer, pp. 77

[5] Graham, The Reno Court of Inquiry, pp. 145-146

[6] Hardorff, The Custer Battle Casualties, II, pp. 100

[7] Barnard, Ten Years With Custer, pp. 304

[8] Francis B. Taunton, Custer's Field, pp. 32; Camp, pp. 80

[9] Ibid, pp. 307

[10] Nichols, Men With Custer, pp. 391

[11] Ibid, pp. 391

Many of the wounded were carried in stretchers between two mules to get them to the steamboat Far West which was waiting at the junction of the Bighorn and Little Bighorn Rivers. Courtesy of LBHBNM

View toward Little Bighorn River from Custer Hill. The wooden stakes mark grave sites. Courtesy of LBHBNM.

Glossary

Adjutant- The assistant of a commanding officer of a regiment.

Aide- An officer on the personal staff of a General or field officer, that receives and distributes his orders.

Ambush- Sudden surprise attack by an enemy from a place of hiding.

Arapaho Indians- A High Plains Indian tribe who were allied with the Sioux and Cheyenne Indians during the Little Bighorn battle.

Arikara (Rees) Indians- Blood enemies of the Sioux. Scouted for the soldiers.

Barricades- Obstructions formed to prevent an enemy's access.

Battalion- Two or more companies of soldiers.

Blacksmith- A person who works with iron.

Brigade- Two or more regiments of soldiers under the command of a brigadier general.

Brevet- A term used to express promotion by honor. Used during an age when there were very few medals to be awarded. Brevet ranks were usually only used as honorary titles.

Bugle-Calls- The sounds of the bugle or trumpet used in the field or garrison, where voices would be useless to convey commands.

Canteen- A tin or wooden vessel in which soldiers carry water in the field.

Campaign- A military expedition.

Cavalry- Horse soldiers.

Cheyenne Indians- Two distinct bands (Northern and Southern) of Plains Indian tribe. They were allied with the Sioux and Arapaho Indians.

Column- A body of soldiers in deep file and narrow front (usually one to four men), used to move troops in a hurry from one location to another. Columns could be formed in single file, two or four abreast.

Company- A body of men consisting of two platoons, usually consisting of sixty to one hundred men.

Commander- The officer in charge.

Counting Coups- The act of touching an enemy with a hand or a weapon. Many Indian tribes believed it took greater courage to be the first or second person to touch a live or dead enemy that it did to kill.

Cover- Protection from enemy bullets, arrows or spears.

Detachment- A number of men sent out from the main body of soldiers.

Farrier- A person who puts iron shoes on horses.

First Sergeant- The senior sergeant in a company.

Flank- Position along the extreme right or left side of a line. To attack from the side or flank of an opponent.

Formation- The arrangement of soldiers according to prescribed rules.

Garrison- A unit's home fort or base.

Guidon- A cavalry flag or banner.

Infantry- Foot soldiers.

Line- The arrangement of troops in a wide front or battle array.

Militia- A military force raised from the civilian population and helping a regular army.

Non-Commissioned Officers- Sergeants and corporals placed in charge of other enlisted men.

Oblique- To move forward diagonally to the right or left, according to the word of command.

Packer- Civilian hired to help load the pack mules for traveling.

Pack Train- Supply column consisting of mules carrying supplies on pack saddles.

Perimeter- Outer boundary of a defensive position.

Picket Pin- Wooden or iron stakes driven into the earth and attached to a cavalry horse by a rope. Used to confine a cavalry horse to its proper position and to keep it from running away.

Platoon- One half of a company.

Rally- To reform and reorganize troops that have become disordered or scattered.

Range- Distance obtainable by bullets or other projectiles.

Ranks- Military titles that denote position or authority within an organization. In a cavalry unit in order from lowest to highest: Private, Farrier, Blacksmith, Bugler or Trumpeter, Corporal, Sergeant, First Sergeant, Chief Bugler or Trumpeter, Quartermaster-Sergeant, Sergeant-Major, Second Lieutenant, First Lieutenant, Adjutant, Captain, Major, Lieutenant Colonel, Colonel and General.

Ravine- A deep narrow gorge or canyon.

Rear Guard- A group of men who bring up the rear on a march for the purpose of protecting the rear of the main body or formation from enemy attack.

Reconnaissance- The act of scouting an enemy's location.

Reform- To bring a unit to its natural order by aligning it on a given point.

Regiment (cavalry) - Twelve companies of cavalry.

Reserve- Troops retained in the rear of an army to support the attacking force or to rally it in case of disaster.

Retreat- The withdrawal or evacuation of troops. To flee or escape.

Rout- To retreat or flee in an uncontrolled manner.

Scouts- Men hired to gain intelligence of the forces, location and movements of an enemy.

Sioux Indians- Large Northern Plains Indian tribe allied with the Cheyenne and Arapaho against the Army.

Skirmish- Minor fight or battle.

Skirmishers- A small body of men used to fight or engage the enemy, often used to clear an area of the enemy.

Skulker- A person who secretly steals from other people or stays out of sight.

Squad- Four cavalrymen; part of a platoon.

Subaltern- An officer under the rank of captain that aids in the command of a company of soldiers.

Tactics- The arrangement and formation of troops by means of maneuvers and evolutions (movements and turns).

Travois- A stretcher made of two poles connected by blankets, animal hides, tree branches or rope. The connecting material forms a basket which can be used to carry supplies, property or injured people. They are usually towed behind a horse or mule.

Troop- A term used to denote a company of cavalry.

Index

American Horse, 107
Bennett, Private James C., 155
Benteen, Captain Frederick W., 1, 29, 30, 34, 58, 59, 63, 64, 65, 66, 67, 68, 69, 71, 76, 79, 103, 114, 115, 116, 117, 120, 121, 122, 126, 127, 128, 133, 134, 135, 136, 137, 139, 141, 147, 150, 151
Bloody Knife, 24, 25, 33, 42, 45
Bobo, First Sergeant Edwin, 88
Bob-Tailed Bull, 25, 39, 40
Botzer, Sergeant Edward, 44
Boyer, Mitch, 12, 26, 57, 68, 75, 76
Boyle, Private James P., 43
Bradley, Lieutenant James H., 144, 147, 148
Brennan, Private John, 57
Camp, Walter M., 119
Contrary Belly, 87
Crazy Horse, 87, 91, 92, 101, 107
Crook, General George, 31, 32, 146
Crow King, 107
Crow's Nest, 23, 25, 26
Curly, 58, 69, 75, 76, 151
Curtiss, Sergeant William A., 25, 26
Custer, Boston, 59, 64, 65, 76, 80
Custer, Bvt Major General George Armstrong, 4, 5, 15, 16, 17, 23, 24, 25, 26, 27, 28, 29, 30, 32, 33, 41, 56, 57, 58, 63, 65, 66, 67, 68, 69, 71, 75, 76, 77, 78, 79, 147, 149, 150
Custer, Captain Thomas Ward, 58, 59, 66, 80, 102, 149, 153, 155
Deeds, 32
DeRudio, Lieutenant Charles C., 37, 45, 119, 142
DeWolf, Dr. James M., 44, 45
Dorman, Isaiah, 45, 46, 143
Dose, Trumpeter Henry C., 80
Dull Knife, 107
Edgerly, Lieutenant Winfield Scott, 69, 115, 116, 121
Finckle, Sergeant George August, 86
Finley, Sergeant Jeremiah, 77, 78, 86
French, Captain Thomas Henry, 15, 28, 47, 126, 135
Gerard, Frederic F., 25, 32, 33, 99, 119, 142
Gibbon, Colonel John, 129, 146, 147, 152
Gibson, Lieutenant Francis M., 63, 152

Godfrey, Lieutenant Edward
  Settle, 29, 34, 70, 114, 118,
  121, 122, 131, 148, 157, 158
Goes Ahead, 68
Goldin, Private Theodore W., 34
Gordon, Private Henry, 44
Hairy Moccasin, 68
Hanley, Sergeant Richard P., 126
Hare, Lieutenant Luther R., 33,
  38, 39, 70, 115, 116, 147
Harrington, Lieutenant Henry
  Moore, 31, 78, 87, 151
Harrison, Sergeant Thomas W.,
  121
Hodgson, Lieutenant Benjamin H.,
  28, 42, 44, 114, 141
Hughes, Sergeant Robert H., 80
Iron Thunder, 107
Jackson, William, 33, 119, 142
Kanipe, Sergeant Daniel, 56, 58,
  59, 65, 66, 67, 68
Kellogg, Marcus Henry, 80, 99
Keogh, Captain Myles Walter, 1,
  4, 30, 33, 75, 76, 77, 78, 79,
  80, 83, 84, 85, 86, 87, 88, 92,
  93, 94, 99, 100, 103, 104, 106,
  150
Korn, Private Gustave, 120, 138
Lame White Man, 93, 107
Lattman, Private John, 43
Little Brave, 25
Little Hawk, 86, 88

Little Wolf, 26, 76
Long Road, 135
Lord, Dr. George Edwin, 80, 151
Low, Lieutenant, 129
Madden, Saddler Michael P., 137
Mann, Frank C., 134, 143
Martin, Trumpeter John, 58, 59,
  65, 67, 68, 71, 119, 128, 133,
  146
Mathey, Lieutenant Edward
  Gustave, 27, 66, 67
McDougall, Captain Thomas
  Mower, 28, 66, 67, 70, 115,
  117, 120, 126
McIlhargey, Private Archibald, 33
McIntosh, Lieutenant Donald, 28,
  43, 152
Medicine Tail Ford, 58, 75, 76,
  77, 104, 148
Meyer, Private William D., 38, 44
Mitchell, Private John Edward, 33
Morris, Private William E., 41, 43
Moylan, Captain Myles, 28, 38,
  42, 120
Neely, Private Frank, 41
Noisy Walking, 93
O'Hara, Sergeant Miles F., 40
O'Neill, Private Thomas F, 119,
  142
Porter, Dr. Henry R., 122, 137
Porter, Lieutenant James E., 151
Rapp, Private John, 43

Red Star, 24, 25
Reed, Harry Armstrong, 64, 80
Reily, Lieutenant William Van Wyck, 150
Reno, Major Marcus, 4, 5, 28, 29, 30, 31, 32, 33, 37, 40, 41, 42, 45, 46, 47, 48, 56, 57, 58, 59, 60, 63, 64, 65, 66, 68, 69, 70, 71, 72, 75, 76, 77, 80, 84, 107, 114, 115, 116, 117, 118, 119, 120, 122, 123, 126, 127, 128, 129, 130, 131, 133, 135, 136, 138, 140, 141, 142, 143, 146, 147, 148, 152, 153, 158, 164
Reynolds, Charles, 45, 143
Roy, Corporal Stanislas, 131
Rutten, Private Roman, 38
Ryan, First Sergeant John, 15, 39, 136, 143
Sharrow, Sergeant Major William H., 29, 80, 153
Short, Private Nathan, 75
Sitting Bull, 38, 46, 107
Smith, Private George E., 38, 40
Soldier, 57
Standing Bear, 56
Sturgis, Lieutenant James Garland, 100, 151
Summers, Private David, 42
Tanner, Private James, 135
Taylor, Muggins, 147
Taylor, Private William O., 131, 143, 147
Terry, General Alfred H., 18, 75, 76, 129, 130, 140, 141, 146, 147, 148, 151
Thompson, Private Peter, 18, 57, 120, 138
Turning Bear, 32
Two Eagles, 83
Two Moon, 88, 107
Varden, First Sergeant Frank E., 88
Varnum, Lieutenant Charles A., 23, 24, 25, 26, 33, 44, 130, 142, 147
Vickory, Sergeant John, 80
Voight, Private Henry C., 134
Voit, Saddler Otto, 139
Voss, Chief Trumpeter Henry, 29, 80
Wallace, Lieutenant George Daniel, 33, 45, 126
Wallace, Private John W., 45
Watson, Private James, 57, 120
Weir Point, 57, 58, 114, 116, 118, 119, 120, 121, 148
Weir, Captain Thomas Benton, 29, 57, 58, 75, 76, 114, 115, 116, 118, 119, 120, 121, 148
Wells, Farrier Benjamin J., 43
White Man Runs Him, 68
White Swan, 33, 45

Windolph, Private Charles A., 139, 143, 144, 149
Wooden Leg, 18, 34, 81, 131
Yates, Captain George W., 25, 31, 76, 77, 78, 79, 80, 99, 100, 104, 106, 150

Yellow Nose, ii, iii, 87
Young Two Moon, 88